C000245854

The People's History
Sunderland
Shipyards

by

Andrew Clark

Copyright © Andrew Clark 1998

First published in 1998
Reprinted in 2002

The People's History Ltd
Suite 1
Byron House
Seaham Grange Business Park
Seaham
Co. Durham
SR7 0PY

ISBN 1 902527 00 3

No part of this publication may be reproduced, stored in a mechanical retrieval system, or transmitted, in any form or by any means, electronic, mechanical, photocopying, recording or otherwise, without prior permission of the author.

Contents

JL Thompson's North Sands football team, 1957. Back row, left to right: John Cook, John Mason, Alfie Farley, Brian Spendley, John Duffy, John Bell, Harry Pearson. Front row: Les 'Bo' Jobling, Tommy Sawyer, Eddie McDermott, Alec Sloanes, Dessie Ellis.

Acknowledgements

I would like to thank all the individuals and organisations who have helped me with this publication.

In particular I appreciate the help and support of Alan Brett, Ian Wright, Billy Dent, Peter Gibson, Alan Owen, Northeast Press and Phil Hall & Ashley Sutherland at Sunderland City Library.

Thanks to Ian S. Carr for his excellent photographs on pages 47, 56 (bottom), 57 (top) and 71.

Bibliography

Alan Brett, *Sunderland People and Places*, 1990
Joe Clarke, Phil Hall, Peter Hepplewhite, Mary Rose, *Sunderland Builds The Ships*, 1989
Peter Gibson, *Southwick-on-Wear Volume 4*, 1996
J. Gordon Holmes, *The Barbary Coast: The Story Of A Community*, 1980
C.H.G. Hopkins, *Pallion 1874 to 1954: Church and People in a Shipyard Parish*, 1954
John Lingwood, *SD14 The Great British Shipbuilding Success Story*, 1976
Norman L. Middlemiss, *British Shipbuilding Yards Volume 1: North-East Coast*, 1993
J.W. Smith & T.S. Holden, *Where Ships Are Born*, 1946

Introduction

My name may be on the cover of this book but I am not the only author of this collection of shipyard stories and photographs. The real credit for this book must go to the many people who have contributed their memories and treasured pictures. These people, many of them former shipyard workers, have been gracious in allowing us to share their part in the story of shipbuilding on the Wear.

This is not a complete history of shipbuilding in Sunderland – that would take many volumes – but a 'people's history' of the town's famous industry. The majority of the book is made up of short stories I have taken from taped interviews but some of the text has also come from other publications – newspapers, books and magazines. I have also included a couple of passages from the famous book *Where Ships Are Born*.

I hope the reader will recognise that time can sometimes distort the memory and some of the people I have spoken to may have confused a few facts. I am sure many readers will say they have stories just as good as the ones in this book. If you have, I would like to hear from you. Already people have asked when I am writing the next book. It just goes to show the fascination we have in shipbuilding in Sunderland. Today we still take pride in the title – 'The biggest shipbuilding town in the World.'

Andrew Clark

This book is dedicated to all those who have been kind enough to share their stories and photographs with the rest of us:

Dave Aldridge, Jim Baldwin, John Banks, Tommy Bell, Bernie Blackwell, Peter Callaghan, Harry Clark, May Cook, Tom Cunningham, Phil Curtis, Billy Dent, Doris Downes, Kenny Downes, Bobby Duckworth, Arthur Dykes, Tommy Fairley, Joe Falcus, Jean Fowler, Stan Fowler, Derek Frost, Holcus (Harry) Gibson, Pearce Gibson, Peter Gibson, Alf Henderson, Audrey Henderson, Ted Howell, John Humphreys, Steve James, Bo Jobling, Billy Johnson, Derek Laidler, Derek Laidler jnr, Edward 'Mac' MacKenzie, Peter Martin, Stu McSween, Jimmy Mullen, George Nairn, Brian Nicholson, Bob Palmer, John Potts, Bryan Rackstraw, Bill Reay, Edith Richardson, Tom Richardson, Doreen Robson, Bob Simpson, Gladys Stephenson, Mary Stephenson, Mickey Stephenson, Andrew Stewart, Ronnie Stubbs, Phil Sydney, Jimmy Taylor, Keith Thomas, Margaret Thynne (formerly Burlinson), Jackie Turnbull, Lily Turnbull, John Yearnshire.

The propeller is fitted to the *Troutbank* at Laing's in 1979.

SHIPYARD LIFE

Living By The River … Family Traditions … Apprenticeship …
Workmates … Social Life … End Of The Day …

The Bowery Boys – Taken on the berth gantry, JL Thompson's, 1968. Left to right: Mattie Snowden, Gordon Reay, Brian Nicholson, Harry Fowler, Larry Clark (standing), Brian Holden, Teddy Metcalfe.

Living By The River

The Barbary Coast

I lived near JL Thompson's most of my life. Opposite the entrance to JL's stood Zetland Street and behind that stood Mulgrave Street where I lived. On the day I started at JL's seven of my mates from Mulgrave Street started with me: Davie Corpus, Bob Lay, Jackie Walker, Brian Nicholson, George Solomon, Bo Jobling and John Tansey and two more from Zetland Street: Billy Potts and John Ramsay. Almost every lad in the neighbouring streets got a start at JL's when they left school in those days. When I got married we lived at Downhill for a short while. I still drank around the Wheatsheaf area and sometimes missed the last bus home and stopped at my mother's in Mulgrave Street. I would then go straight to work in my good clothes.

Billy Dent

Many of JL's workmen lived practically on the yard's doorstep and some would boast that they 'could leave home when the buzzer started blowing and get through the gates before it stopped.' The rush down Zetland Street at 7.30 and 1 o'clock bore this out.

The Barbary Coast streets were the limit of their lives for some of these men. They worked there, took there drinks there, found all their amusements there, and were visited there by their own corner-end 'bookies'.

J. Gordon Holmes, *Sunderland Echo*, 2nd December 1980.

The Barbary Coast – JL Thompson's and the neighbouring streets, *circa* 1940. The rows of streets to the left of the berths supplied the yard with a labour force within a stone's throw of the works' gates. From the top of picture: Millum Place, Normanby Street, Mulgrave Street, Zetland Street, Bloomfield Street, Hardwick Street and Barrington Street.

Workers leave Laing's at the start of the shipyard fortnight holiday, 1979.

When Deptford Was Packed

I lived in Deptford as a young girl and in those days the streets would be packed with people – unlike today. I remember the shipyard workers coming to and from work. Some of them had filthy clothes on and they would be carrying their cans of tea and bait boxes.

Me and my friends would watch the launch of ships from Pickie's on the other side of the river – it was a tremendous sight and I used to love it. We used to stand just up from where Websters is now where there used to be a grassy bank. We would sit on a wall but as the time of the launch got nearer we would move further back because we knew the water would surge over the banks. Sometimes I would watch the launches from the upstairs windows of my school at Deptford Terrace. After the ships were away all the wood in the water would be collected up by the men in little cobles.

Jean Fowler

Childhood Memories

I used to do a paper round in Deptford in the 1950s while still at school. I would see all the workers heading for the shipyards every morning. I would listen for the buzzer to go off for the men to start work and I knew it was 7.30. We lived right on top of the bank leading to the river's edge. When it was low tide us kids would play in all the dirty muck and slime and wave and chat to the shipyard workers on the other side of the river.

Audrey Henderson

Noise Pollution

The shipyards, factories and collieries all had their buzzers. It would be quiet until the buzzer went at 7.30. Then all hell was let loose with the noise of riveters and caulkers. Then at dinner time the noise would stop. Today people would be complaining about the noise but in those days you were used to it and it was like that all over the town.

Stan Fowler

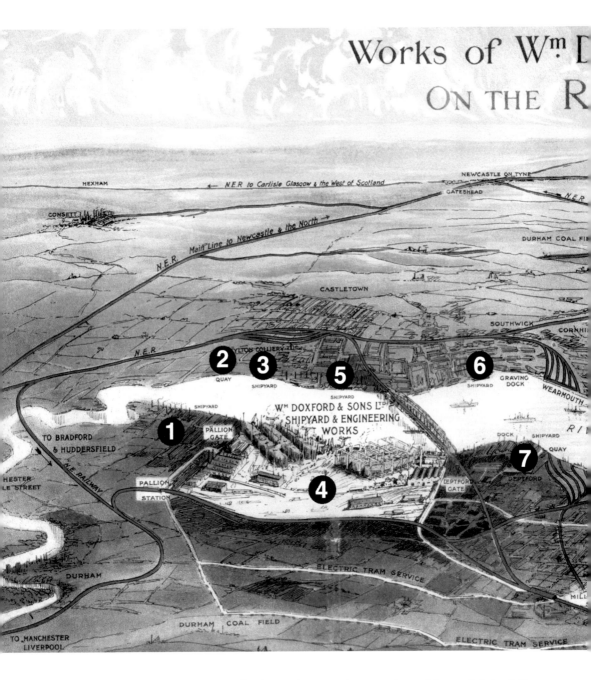

This map – produced by Doxford's – gives an impression of how shipbuilding once dominated the banks of the Wear. We have marked on the shipyards featured in this book:

1. Short's, 2. Corporation Yard, 3. John Priestman's, 4. Doxford's,
5. Pickersgill's, 6. Robert Thompson's, 7. Laing's, 8. Austin's,
9. JL Thompson's, 10 Bartram's.

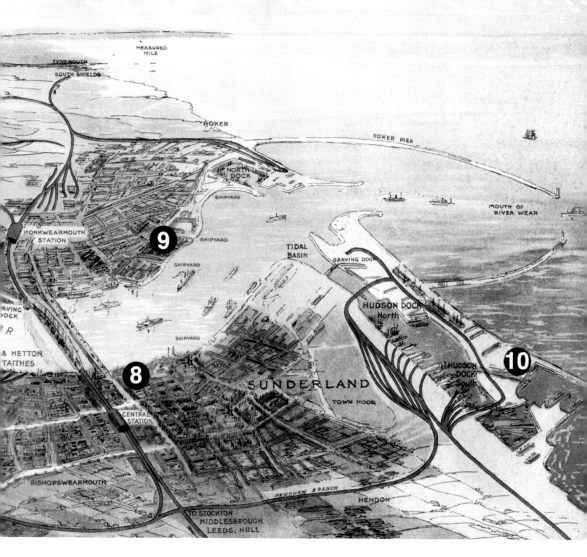

The names of some of the yards changed over the years as various mergers took place. Throughout the book, the author has used the 'traditional' names of the yards – the ones used by the people telling the stories.

Family Traditions

Shipbuilding having been carried on for many generations, it naturally follows that every boy born in the town for generations has listened to the ringing click of the shipwright's mallet in the wooden shipbuilding days, to the music of the hand riveting and caulking tools so common in today's modern shipyards. Hence it is fair to assume that our population, so steeped with the traditions of this industry, by the very nature of things, is eminently adapted for shipyard work. I have known five generations of one family who have worked in Sunderland shipyards.

Sir James Marr, Chairman of Laing's, April 1928.

Like Father Like Son (Almost)

My dad was a good worker. When I followed him into the yard I was told, 'You are not as good as your father, but you will do.'

Tom Richardson

A Great Burner

You had a lot of respect for the good workers in the yards who really knew their trade. If I met someone who had worked with my dad, people would say, 'He was a hell of a burner.'

Alf Henderson

Tom Richardson (right) and a fellow security guard at Austin & Pickersgill's in the late 1970s. Tom ended his working life at Pickersgill's but he started his shipyard career at Doxford's in the 1930s where his dad (Tom senior) was a well-known plater.

Just Like Home

When I started at Laing's in 1959 I had five uncles and two cousins working in the yard. So I was quite at home when I started work. That sort of family connection was common in all the yards. Men followed their dads, uncles or brothers into the shipyards. It was a good thing, especially for discipline, because lads were sometimes frightened about what they did in case they got wrong off their dads or big brothers.

Kenny Downes

The End Of The Line

The Revells were a famous shipyard family whose link with the industry came to an end in 1982. The A&P News paid tribute to Jack Revell on his retirement:

Revell is a name in shipbuilding on the Wear which is as well known as those of the great yard owners. But, after six generations the connection of this Wearside family with the proud industry is to be severed. Jack Revell is retiring due to ill health, aged 63 – the last of the line.

If his father had had his way, the Revell connection would have been ended much sooner. Jack Revell senior had seen his own father, William Thomas Revell, killed while working at Sir James Laing's yard in 1926. He knew the suffering this had brought to the family and forbade his son Jack to go into shipbuilding. Just eight years later, in 1934, the young Jack defied his father's wishes and began work as a marker boy.

At the age of 14, his wage was 4s and 6d for a 47 hour week. He recalls: 'I gave all my wages to my mother and she gave me back 6d a week pocket money. I remember a quarter of boiled sweets cost 1d and sometimes at the end of the week I would still have 1d left – unless my sister had scrounged it off me!'

Jack also has vivid memories of the hardships in the yards in those days. 'Bartram's, of course, was on the seafront. There were no sheds or shelter of any kind. Jobs were few and far between so the men worked hard. If they didn't they would be told to go. There were always men waiting at the yard ready to take their jobs.'

Jack must have had doubts about the job, when in the 1950s, his father was killed in the yards. But he continued, and his career developed from plater, to foreman plater and finally, training supervisor.

'I will certainly miss the yard – it has been my life for so long and I have made some good friends.'

Jack Revell (right) at his retirement presentation, December 1982.

Apprenticeship

Standing On The Market

I started as an apprentice shipwright at Pickersgill's in 1939. In those days you started when you were fourteen. I didn't intend to be a shipwright – I wanted to be an electrician. With a friend, Peter Callaghan, I walked the town looking for work. I went to various places and I put my name down for the Sunderland Forge. The last place I went to was the nearest place to where we lived and that was William Pickersgill's. When we went to Pickersgill's there were two other lads there I knew – Wilfy Harrison and Bobby Masters.

There was four of us standing on the 'Market', as they called it, waiting to see the foreman. You had to stand to attention in those days. He came along and said, 'What do you want?' We said to the foreman that we were looking for work. He said to me, 'Are you any good at woodwork?' I was pretty good at school so he said, 'Start work tomorrow up in the mould loft.' I didn't know what the mould loft was. I hardly knew what a ship was never mind a mould loft. So I ended up in the mould loft and the other lads were out on the berths. The mould loft was where they laid the ship out on the floor in full size and made templates for the plates. I didn't get on very well with the boss up there, Mr Douglas, and so I more or less got thrown out. I had engineered it because I wanted to be out with the other lads on the berths.

Tommy Bell

Left to right: George Grieves, Tommy Bell, Peter Callaghan, Jimmy Holyoak at Pickersgill's in the mid 1950s. Tommy and Peter started work at the yard on the same day in 1939.

This aerial view of three Sunderland shipyards, *circa* 1945, illustrates how industry once dominated the Wear. Young lads leaving school had no problems finding work with so many companies operating in the town. Doxford's is in the foreground, with Pickersgill's on the opposite bank and the Corporation Yard in the top left of the picture. The Corporation Yard was opened during the Second World War on the site of the Swan Hunter's yard which had closed in the early 1930s. In 1942 workers from JL Thompson's re-built three berths and a year later the first ship had been launched. The yard was closed for the final time in 1947.

No Interviews

There weren't many choices for young lads leaving school in my day. You only really had three choices – go to sea, down the pit or in the yards. You normally followed your dad into his trade, so if he worked in the yards that's where you started work. When I started work in the 1940s there were no interviews for jobs. Your dad took you down when you were fifteen and said to the gaffer, 'I've got a boy here who wants a job.' You then started straight away.

Ted Howell

In The Blacksmith's Shop

I started at Austin's straight from school in 1951 in the blacksmith's shop. In those days you knew you would easily get a job, not like it is today. I went down to Austin's with a mate of mine and we met this fella who asked me what I was up to. I said I was going for a catching or heating job. He said, 'Don't be daft, I'll take you to the blacksmith's shop.' There were no personnel managers in those days. I was taken straight to the gaffer who was told, 'He's a young lad, just left school, he needs a bit job.' I started there and then.

Tommy Fairley

On Good Money

My dad and my uncle worked in the shipyards but my first job was at Luxdon Laundry when I was fifteen. Then my Uncle Jack got me into Doxford's. I'd passed my eleven plus so they started me as a clerk. But I liked the yard more and I used to congregate with the lads who worked on the ships. So I asked for another job and I started as a plater. When I finished my apprenticeship I started working with the top platers and I was on good money. I was earning three times the money of my friends who I had done my apprenticeship with. Doxford's was a good yard to learn your trade and I was taught really well.

Alf Henderson

Alf Henderson at Doxford's in the 1960s.

WILLIAM DOXFORD & SONS SHIPBUILDERS LTD · PALLION · SUNDERLAND

Certificate of Apprenticeship

This is to certify that........JOHN ALFRED HENDERSON............

served an apprenticeship as a........PLATER............

with this company from.....8th October....19 60 .to....7th October....19 65

at which date his term of apprenticeship was satisfactorily completed

DATE 8th October, 1965.

MANAGING DIRECTOR

Alf Henderson's certificate of apprenticeship from Doxford's.

My First Wage

My first wage in September 1966 was £3 2s 7d (£3.13) to take home. Out of that was £2 board to my mother which left £1 2s 7d pocket money. One of my friends had a job in a cafe and others worked as labourers and their take home pay was twice as much as mine. But that, I suppose, was the sacrifice we apprentices had to make before we came into the 'big money' when we came out of our time. The big money carrot was more like a big joke as apprentices at that time continued to be used as a cheap source of labour.

Peter Gibson

Apprentices at Austin & Pickersgill's in 1981. Left to right: Kevin Marshall, Gary Lacy, Michael Taylor.

Workmates

Comradeship

Bartram's was a real family yard. My father worked there before me and I automatically followed him into the yard and many other men did exactly the same. There was a very friendly atmosphere and you knew everybody and there was a feeling of camaraderie. I don't miss the work but I miss the companionship. Nearly every time I walk through the town there is someone I bump into who I worked with and we stop and have a talk about the old days. You don't get that camaraderie at work these days. We would socialise together and on launch days we would have a few beers and enjoy ourselves.

Ronnie Stubbs

The Boilerhouse Barber

If you wanted your haircut at Laing's you went down to the boilerhouse. There was a lad there who only charged sixpence and you got a nice haircut.

Ed MacKenzie

Dinner Time Rush

It was a real rush at dinner time at Doxford's so we would get our meals together. One lad would get the soup, one the dinners, one the sweets. When the bell went and they opened the doors of the canteen everyone was away and you had to run. You would see people falling and others jumping over them. The queues were massive.

Alf Henderson

Men at Doxford's, including: Billy Shanks, Les Wilson, Dave Richmond, Stan Peacock, Ralph Alsop.

Pocket Money

At Thompson's there was Pa Kemp and his five boilermaker sons. One of them, Tommy, rewarded apprentices who worked with him with 10 shillings pocket money. That was a good boost to an apprentice's wage packet.

Peter Gibson

Football Daft

Tommy Lloyd was a plumber at Laing's in the 1950s and he was mad about football. One day he slept in and never got to work but when the lads came out at dinner time to play football Tommy was waiting outside the gates for them. After the match the lads went back to work and Tommy went home.

Jimmy Mullen

Bartram's men enjoy a night out in the 1970s.

The Sand Dancers

We had some men down at Bartram's who we called the 'sand dancers'. With Bartram's being on the South Dock we had trouble with sand being brought in by the tide every day. So these lads, the sand dancers, had to shovel the sand away. They had to do this every day.

Ted Howell

Serving Your Workmates

I decided to be a shop steward because I wanted to serve the people I worked with. I wanted to contribute and I had ideas about how conditions could be improved. I'm proud to say I was a shop steward for thirteen years and we had elections every year and I was elected each time. It gave me the feeling that I must have had the respect of my fellow workmen. It was nice to be part of a team that saw the evolvement of better working conditions, safety or wages. I can look back and say I did contribute – not that it's any good now with the yards gone.

Kenny Downes

Ladies In The Yards

Happy Times At Doxford's

When I left school in 1944, I started work as a junior tracer in the engineering office at Doxford's earning 25 shillings a week. Another junior started work the following week making five of us together with the senior tracer – an elderly lady nearing retirement age – Miss Wright.

We were advised to join the union hoping to get the Saturday morning off. The following year the Second World War ended, the Labour Government came to power and sure enough we got the Saturday mornings off, as well as two weeks annual holiday instead of one week, a 42 hour working week and all Bank Holidays. It was all very exciting.

There were seven tracers by then and a busy drawing office downstairs. There were regular launches and all the other shipyards were busy too – the River Wear was thriving.

Doreen Robson (née Tindle), aged sixteen in 1945.

I'll always remember the daily noise of the shipyards. It was like a massive dawn chorus or an orchestra of sounds, suddenly increasing in volume after 7.30 am with the riveters, platers and welders all going 'hammer and tongs'. Once when I was staying with my aunt at Southwick, I missed the bus to Pallion and had to walk over Alexandra Bridge at 9 o'clock in the morning.

Doreen Fenwick, a tracer at Doxford's, 1945.

The noise was deafening, coming from all sides and although it was exhilarating in a way, it was nice to get into the peace and safety of the office.

The crowds were amazing as well. They were just like football match days – but like that everyday. When I was a young mother, with a three-year-old and a young baby, I had to cancel my daughter's tea-time dance classes, held in a house at the Wheatsheaf, after only three or four lessons as I had forgotten about the shipyard crowds at 5 o'clock. I lived on the other side of the town then. It was very difficult to walk with the pram over Wearmouth Bridge and impossible to get on a bus at St Mary's Church.

You had to have your coats and skirts continually cleaned or washed after being on a bus or tram that the shipyards workers had been travelling on. They usually wore the same clothes and overalls all the week so they were pretty oily and dusty by the weekend. There were no automatic washing machines in those days.

I was very happy at Doxford's and loved the work. There was a bit of friendly rivalry among the girls, but the older ones helped us a lot and Miss Wright was a good boss – quiet but firm. There was great satisfaction in our work. The pale blue waxed linen, chalked and stretched, then traced with Black Indian Ink, was a treat to behold when done carefully. We were as proud of our tracings, which could take days or even weeks to do, as the draughtsmen themselves must have been with the detailed drawings they had given us to trace. It was lovely to see the first huge prints come out of the printing machine. The most difficult one I remember to trace was called a Bilge and Ballast. It took over seven weeks to trace and I was really glad to see it completed.

The pay for us was dismal though, £3 a week at nineteen years of age. When my friend, Doreen Fenwick, who was a year younger than I was, left to start work nearby for £6 a week, twice my salary, I must admit it unsettled me. I lived with my aunt and although she was good to me, I wanted to pay my board and feel independent. I applied for a job at a nearby engineering works. I was £1 better off a week, not as good as my friend's pay packet, but I took it all the same. Mr J. Hardy, the chief draughtsman of Doxford's was a lovely man and so was his assistant Mr J. Gunn, but they couldn't do much about my wages.

Looking back, I was very lucky because both firms were good places to work for. We also had good bosses who took care of their staff.

Doreen Robson

Women at work in a Sunderland shipyard during the Second World War.

A Tracer's Story

All my family were brought up in Southwick near to Austin & Pickersgill's. In those days families always lived near to each other. My grandparents, Hannah and Joseph Green, had the shop which was outside the yard. My grandfather had a terrible fall at George Clark's Engine Works and was paralysed and spent the rest of his life in a wheelchair. He got £100 compensation and with that money they opened the shop. One of my mam's sisters and her children lived in the Times Inn. My mam and dad lived in Clockwell Street which is now demolished.

My father, Ossie Church, worked at George Clark's Engine Works in the Pattern Shop and he was well-known for being a good worker. When I was fifteen I wanted to be a nurse but on the Friday I left school I came home and my dad said to me, 'I've got you a job as a tracer at George Clark's, you start on Monday.'

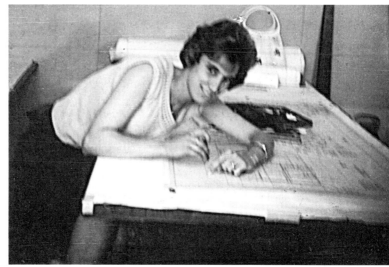

Doris Downes (née Church) at work at George Clark's Engine Works in 1961.

I didn't even know what a tracer was. At that time if you didn't like a job you could leave and start somewhere else straight away so I thought I would try it. I didn't even have an interview – I just started at 9 o'clock the following Monday. I stayed, finished my apprenticeship and loved the job.

There were six tracers in our office working on plans produced by about thirty draughtsmen. We worked on desks which were six to eight feet long. The draughtsmen would do the drawings on very long rolls and then they would come down to us. Sometimes it would take three months to trace one drawing. The head tracer would check our work and then the plans would be used.

I also worked at North East Marine and when I finished my apprenticeship I got a job at Austin & Pickersgill's. It was easier at Pickersgill's because the plans were for ships whereas at George Clark's the plans were for engines which were more detailed.

I married Kenny, a welder at Pickersgill's. When Kenny was giving his speech at the wedding he said, 'I'm the talk of the welding department – a welder marrying a commoner – a tracer.' In 1963 I fell pregnant which was the end of my time in the yards. In those days you couldn't go part-time and they didn't keep your job for you while you were on maternity leave so I had to finish working. I have never worked as a tracer since.

Doris Downes

Canteen Lady

I started work in the canteen at Austin & Pickersgill's in 1977 expecting to stay for three weeks but stopped for six years. We had a good union woman who fought for kitchen staff to have the same wages as labourers in the yard and we were on good money. After Sunderland Shipbuilders took over we sometimes worked in the canteen at Doxford's. I took my redundancy a few years before the yards closed.

Gladys Stephenson

The Austin & Pickersgill's canteen staff Christmas dinner, 1984. On the right is Mary Stephenson whose husband, Tommy, was a shipyard painter.

Hard Work At Bartram's

I started work in Bartram's canteen in the early 1930s, not long after leaving school. The food for the men was cooked in large boiler-like containers. Our boss was an old battle-axe who had us on our hands and knees scrubbing the floors at weekends.

Lily Turnbull

I Name This Ship

When I worked at Pickie's I would watch all the launches – I once shook hands with Princess Margaret when she came to the yard. Sometimes, if they didn't have anyone to launch a ship, the names of all the women in the yard would be put into a hat and the one picked out would launch the ship. I was never lucky enough to be picked.

Doris Downes

The Workers

What's A Welder?

I was introduced into the yard by my Uncle Fred Watts. He said, 'I'm going to get you a start as an apprentice welder.'

I said, 'What's a welder?'

'Welding is the job to be in', he said, 'That's where the money is.' It was a growing trade at that time as it was taking over from riveting.

In the 1950s the riveter squads were the kings. One would heat the rivet, another would throw it up, the catcher caught it and put it in the hole, the riveter worked one side with the holder up on the other. If you got in their way they would quickly get you out of the road. I was a welder and I remember my welding screen being kicked away. You were nothing to them. It was at the time riveters were starting to be phased out and welders were a threat to them. They thought their world wouldn't be taken over by welding. As it happened most of them became tack welders.

Kenny Downes

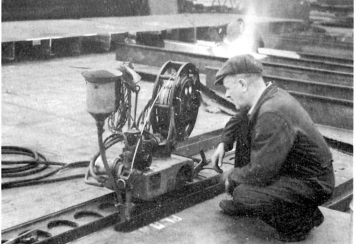

Above: A deck prepared for riveting at Pickersgill's in the early 1950s. The photograph was taken by Tom Cunningham who was a welder at Pickersgill's and a keen amateur photographer.

Left: A Fusarc welding machine in action at Doxford's.

Shipwrights positioning a shore under the shell bottom. One shipwright steadies the shore while the other uses the maul to knock in wood wedges.

Easy Life

When I started at Pickersgill's in 1939 there were only two welders. They were two ex-miners. Then they brought another one in and so one was made chargeman. These welders could name their own price for the job. I used to work on Saturday afternoons to site the keels to see how the ship was standing on the berth.

One Saturday at lunch time the welders went away at 12 o'clock to get their dinner and didn't come back till 2 o'clock. The chap I was working with said, 'They get more for five minutes than I get for the afternoon.' The money they got was out of this world.

I wouldn't say you got a better ship if it was welded. I think you got a better shape if it was riveted.

Tommy Bell

A Condor computer controlled burning machine being operated at Austin & Pickersgill's, *circa* 1970.

Men from the plumbers' shop at Laing's enjoy a dance at the Barnes Hotel with their wives and girlfriends in the 1950s.

Boom Or Bust

When a ship was being fitted-out there was a glut of work for trades like joiners, plumbers, electricians and fitters. Many of the extra men employed were labourers. Once a ship was finished and it was a slack period you were paid off.

Bob Palmer

You Couldn't Beat Experience

Your managers worked their way up from tradesmen. If you were a good tradesmen you went on to be a foreman or a manager. In the latter years they brought in graduates or new people who had never worked in the yards before. They might have had their degrees but they just didn't have the experience.

Alf Henderson

Shipyard painters in the 1960s. Tommy Stephenson (second from right) worked at Laing's and JL Thompson's, becoming a foreman painter.

In 1969 Alan Owen submitted *The History of Education and Training of Apprentices in the Shipbuilding Industry in Sunderland* for a Diploma in Advanced Educational Studies at the University of Newcastle. This included the table below which lists the workers employed by all Sunderland shipbuilding and ship repairing firms in November 1965.

Staff Employees	Males	Females
Scientists and technologists (including engineers)	65	
Designers/draughtsmen/tracers	165	12
Other staff technicians	81	
Secretarial, typing & clerical staff	64	98
Other administrative and commercial staff	108	5
Other staff	44	25
Skilled Workers		
Blacksmiths	67	
Boilermakers	19	
Brass finishers	13	
Caulkers/burners	383	
Coppersmiths	6	
Drillers	83	
Electrical and maintenance electricians	100	
Fitters and maintenance fitters	90	
Fitters and turners	39	
Holder on	16	
Joiners	439	
Machinists	4	
Millwrights	26	
Moulder and coremakers	17	
Painters	133	
Patternmakers	1	
Platers	567	
Plumbers	238	
Polishers	17	
Riggers	15	
Riveters	25	
Sheet iron and sheet metal workers	1	
Shipfitters	183	
Shipwrights, including loftsmen	568	
Tinsmiths	3	
Turners	3	
Welders	1077	
Woodcutting machinists and sawyers	17	
Other skilled workers	6	
Apprentices not yet allocated a skill	141	
Supervisors not allocated elsewhere	16	2
Semi-skilled workers	1191	
Unskilled workers	1028	70
Total	7059	212

The tools of three generations of the Thomas family.

Above: Leslie Thomas was a shipwright at JL Thompson's from just before the Second World War until the late 1970s. Leslie followed his father into the yards and used tools handed down by his dad. *Right:* Leslie's son, Keith Thomas outside his picture frame shop in Pallion. Like many former shipyard men, Keith's new vocation is far removed from his former employment.

Social Life

A Grand Night

The welders at JL Thompson's used to book a function room at the old Grand Hotel in Bridge Street for their Christmas party. Hundreds of us were packed in every year. As the drink flowed things always got a bit boisterous. Lads wandered into areas of the hotel they shouldn't have been in. The management used to say it will never happen again and barred us. But each year we were back and the same things happened.

Billy Dent

Right: The Grand Hotel in Bridge Street. The fifty room hotel was opened in the 1880s and was finally closed in 1969.

Shipyard men and their wives enjoy a night out in the 1970s. Pickersgill's men Stan James (left) and Kenny Downes (right) are in the foreground. Stan moved away from Sunderland to find work when the yards closed. He now lives in Newport but regularly returns to his home town to see family and friends.

Men at Bartram's enjoy a party on the last nightshift before the start of the Christmas break in the mid 1970s. Included are: John Mulvaney (Big Mul), Joe Nichol, John Bell and Davie Hudson.

The Family Yard

Bartram's was a happy yard with the workers one big happy family. But there was a lot of hard graft as well. It was a pleasure to work in the yard even though there was nothing modern in it. But despite the working conditions we still built six or seven ships a year when we were working on the SD14s. I would go back tomorrow if they opened it up.

Ted Howell

The William Pile pub, on the corner of Dame Dorothy Street and Zetland Street, was named after the famous nineteenth century shipbuilder. William Pile was called a shipbuilding genius. This pub was one of many in Sunderland whose names had shipyard links. Others included; the Boilermakers' Arms, the Shipwrights' Arms, The Slipway and The Torrens.

Stu McSween behind the bar of the Howard Arms in Roker Avenue.

Welding To Pub Life

I started at Austin & Pickersgill's in the mid 1970s as an apprentice welder. We were boys amongst men but the tradesmen you were working with took you under their wing. There were great characters in the yards in those days and it was a pleasure to go to work. After ten years I took my redundancy. Many of the characters had already left and it was not the same.

I went into the pub trade shortly after leaving the yards. I worked in the Dun Cow and the Beehive before moving to the Howard Arms in Roker Avenue. There are a lot of old shipyard lads get into the Howard Arms and the other pubs in the Avenue.

Stu McSween

The Upper Deck

On Monday afternoons in the '70s and '80s the Upper Deck pub, above the Market Square, used to be packed with shipyard lads. Some had left the yards but met in the pub to have a drink with old mates. Others were taking a half day. A few were on their dinner break but after a couple of pints decided to stay out. I remember one day a welder from Laing's decided to stop with his mates instead of going back. When we left the pub his welder's mitt was stuck in the hat stand. From the Upper Deck we usually moved on to the Dun Cow because it had a bookies next door.

Like the shipyards, the Upper Deck is no longer there. It closed when the roof was put on The Bridges shopping centre and even the Dun Cow has a new trendy Irish name.

Jackie Turnbull

Sporting Life

All Sports Except Badminton

We used to pay a penny a week to go to the TLF (Thompson's, Laing's and Forge) Club in Fulwell. I would run from my house at 14 Deptford Road, over Gill Bridge to Fulwell. We used to play football, cricket, snooker or table tennis but it was normally only the office staff who were allowed to play badminton. International table tennis players came to the TLF for exhibition matches. There was also a sailing club for the apprentices. It was amazing for a young lad like me who had come from a hard life in an orphanage to experience things like this.

Ed MacKenzie

Apprentice tracers at a sports day at the TLF Club in the 1940s.

From Schooldays To Workdays

In 1956 I left school on a Friday, went for a job at JL Thompson's the following day (Saturday) and started work on the Monday. The man doing the interviewing was an old army major called Mr Charlton and all he asked was, 'Can you play football?' (JL's had a great football team at the time.) I said 'yes' and he said, 'Start on Monday.'

Billy Dent

A Grand Ground

The TLF ground had some of the best pitches in the town. The groundsman wouldn't let you play if it was raining. I think at one time Sunderland football club wanted to buy the pitches for their training ground.

Billy Johnson

Laing's Apprentice football team in 1963 – the year they won the YOC Apprentice League Cup. Back row, left to right: Kenny Downes, Jimmy Shanks, Derek Hargreaves, Billy Storey, Tommy McIntosh, Derek Stephenson. Front row: - Graham, Bryan Rackstraw, Brian Purvis, Maurice Wood, Peter Stevenson. The photograph was taken on Doxfields, the home pitch of Doxford's, with the Greyhound Stadium in the background.

Austin & Pickersgill's cricket team, 1982. The team played in the North East Durham League and the photograph was taken on the A&P sports ground which was formerly Bartram's ground. The Whitburn site was taken over by Sunderland football club and is now named the Charlie Hurley Centre.

Right: Thompson's 'B' team – The unbeaten Wearside Apprentices' League and knockout cup winners, 1970-71. Front row, left to right: Geordie Rooks, Billy Burns, Keith Blackett, Joe Dagg, Mickey Conlin, Jimmy Smith. Back row: - Gibbons, Tommy - , Peter Gibson, Arthur Wright, Bobby Burns, Pat Tansey. One player who is not on the photograph is Derek Jones.

Happy Days

The highlight of my apprenticeship was playing football for the yard team in the Wearside Apprentices' League. It perhaps gives some idea of the size of industry on Wearside in the late '60s and early '70s when a league of apprentices contained fourteen teams. Some firms like Thompson's had two teams. Thompson's produced some good apprentice teams over the years and I had the good fortune to play in two very successful sides. They were happy days as we pushed for the league and league knockout cup. The talk leading up to Saturday morning fixtures and the analysis in the yard the following Monday created a good working atmosphere and the games were something to look forward to. In the 1968-69 season I played for Thompson's 'A'. We were defeated only once – in the league cup final replay. The squad that season was: Gibson, Wilson, Carney, Hanson, Higgins, Harle, Thornton, Baines, Smith, Hutchinson, Jones, Brennan and Thompson. Thompson's 'B' team of the 1970-71 season went one better and were unbeaten in the league and were cup winners. Training in those days seemed to be restricted to a game of football outside the yard during the dinner hour. For some this was their cup final and the matches were keenly contested. Hard tackles were put in using steel toe capped work boots. On one occasion I was on the receiving end of an Albert Kemp special which must have resembled a wrestling drop kick rather than a tackle. He caught me squarely on the shoulder with the flat of his boot.

Peter Gibson

Hard Games

When I was an apprentice at Doxford's we would play football every dinner time at Diamond Hall tip. It was sometimes welders against platers and so there were some really tough games. You would think we were playing for the European Cup. You were sweating by the time you got back to work. The next day it was exactly the same.

Alf Henderson

A Footballing Electrician

Sunderland footballer Billy Bingham served his electrician's apprenticeship at Pickersgill's. Billy Parker, who was a director at Sunderland, was also our company secretary and he got him installed at Pickersgill's as an apprentice electrician. Bingham was very slight and very small so he asked his foreman for some weights to build himself up. We made him some weights in the yard. During his break he would go to the back of the electrician's shop and pump iron. He went on to play for Northern Ireland and was their manager for a lot of years.

Tommy Bell

A cartoon from the *Football Echo*, 11th April 1953.

Nineteen-year-old Billy Bingham arrives on Wearside in 1950. Within a few years the Irish winger was established at Roker and was regularly playing for the Northern Ireland side. The youngster's football progress was helped by extra training while an apprentice at Pickersgill's.

Brathay Hall

Apprentices from the TLF Club would go to the outward-bounds centre called Brathay Hall near Lake Windermere. I went in the mid 1950s and we went hill walking, were taught sailing and even time was spent drawing and painting the beautiful scenes around us.

The only bad thing was that at 6.30 in the morning we had to go for a swim in Lake Windermere. It must be the coldest lake in Britain – and you were blue with cold when you got out.

Ed MacKenzie

Brathay Hall, Lake Windermere.

Mixing With Other Lads

I went to Brathay Hall for a month in 1961 and there were other working lads from all over the country. There was half a dozen apprentices from Sunderland and as soon as we got there we were put into different dormitories to encourage us to mix with other lads. You couldn't stay with your mates. I didn't like it at first but by the end of the month I was mixing with lads from Sussex, Manchester and Whitley Bay.

We did various outdoor activities including walking on the fells – sometimes in atrocious conditions. You gradually stopped out for longer periods until by the end of the month we had to stay out on the fells for three days.

The only thing I didn't enjoy was going sailing on the lake. Water and me do not mix – and that's after spending most of my working life on ships.

Kenny Downes

Kenny Downes enjoying himself during his time at Brathay Hall in 1961.

Royal Visits

The visit of George V and Queen Mary to JL Thompson's in June 1917.

The King and Queen visited Sunderland on 15th June 1917, touring Laing's, Doxford's, JL Thompson's, Pickersgill's and John Crown's. The Sunderland Echo reported their visit to Laing's:

The first place visited in the works was the joinery shop, where there were engaged men, young women and girls on various machines.

As the King and Queen moved away they passed along a line of female munition workers, some in cloak overalls and others in trousers. Of several of the girls her Majesty asked how they liked their work and they answered, 'It is very nice.'

In another department of the works the Royal Party witnessed the process of frame-turning. Here is employed at the furnaces Walter Moffatt Fairgrieve, who is in his 82nd year and during 60 years as furnaceman at the yard has never lost a quarter. Only for two short periods, the first as a result of an accident, and the second due to the closing of the yard, has he been absent from his arduous duties.

The Prince

I once met Prince Charles when he came to Doxford's in the 1970s. We spent three days cleaning the yard. They had all the labourers working overtime. It was more like a hotel than a shipyard. Everyone had their orders about what to do when he was in the yard. I had to wait in the fabrication shed and mark this big panel to show him how it was done. I shook hands with him and he asked me what I thought of the new yard which had recently been opened.

Alf Henderson

A Canny Bairn

The Queen first visited Sunderland on 30th April 1946 when she was then Princess Elizabeth. Her duties that day included opening the Eye Infirmary and launching the *Princess Elizabeth* at Laing's. The *Sunderland Echo* reported one incident that day:

'Yer a canny bairn, God bless you', said a woman who stepped out of the crowd lining Queen Alexandra Road as the Princess drove by in her car. The Princess was both amused and pleased at the greeting. She told the Mayor she needed no interpreter to understand its meaning.

The visit of the heir to the thrown was a great occasion for Wearsiders still recovering from the Second World War. Her six mile route from the railway station to the Eye Infirmary and then on to Laing's shipyard was lined with cheering crowds despite the pouring rain.

The future Queen at Laing's for the launch of the *British Princess* in 1946.

The *Echo* reported the scene at Laing's:

A crowd of over 6,000, under a sea of umbrellas, were in the shipyard of Sir James Laing & Sons, Ltd, this afternoon to see Princess Elizabeth launch the firm's 770th vessel, the *British Princess*.

More than half an hour before the vessel left the ways, workmen clambered on to cranes and machinery overlooking the berth. Some even used the new vessel, *Empire Naseby*, fitting out at Laing's quayside as a vantage point.

The Princess walked through the yard amid terrific cheering. She was carrying a bouquet of red roses and smiled and waved to the workmen en route.

As soon as she reached the launching platform workmen began to knock away the first chocks beneath the vessel. Five minutes before the launch was due the *British Princess* was leaving the stocks, having been named by the Princess with these words:

'I name this vessel the *British Princess*. May God bless her and all who sail in her.'

There was a round of cheering as the vessel glided swiftly down the ways and gracefully entered the water.

Mr W.B. Marr (Chairman of Laing's) led a round of cheering in which the workmen joined as they scrambled to collect pieces of the bottle used in the naming ceremony as souvenirs.

Workmen threw their hats into the air as she entered the Wear. The sirens and buzzers of ships in the river sounded in a triumphant chorus.

After the launch the Princess continued the royal tradition of meeting the youngest apprentice at the yard. Jimmy Mackel, only fourteen, was presented to the Princess. The *Echo* reported:

Jimmy, who started as an apprentice plater in December lives at 2 Holylake Square. Seen before the ceremony, he seemed thrilled at the idea of meeting the Princess.

'How long have you been on this job?' asked the Princess.

'Since December', he replied.

'Yours must be a very interesting job', added the Princess.

While travelling through Sunderland by car, passing crowds of people, Princess Elizabeth said to the Mayor, Councillor J. Ritson, 'How well and healthy they look.'

The Mayor replied, 'They have to be healthy to stand this climate.'

Prince Philip at JL Thompson's in 1963.

Retirement

Security Officer Tom Richardson (centre) with personnel staff of Austin & Pickersgill's, on his retirement on 30th January 1981. Tommy was presented with an electric drill from fellow security man Jack Kendrew. Shop steward Alan Turner gave Tom a cheque on behalf of his fellow workmates.

Tom's retirement letter read

Dear Mr Richardson,

On behalf of the Company and all it's employees, I wish to extend to you congratulations on your retirement and express gratitude for the years of service you have given to the firm.

This company has always maintained a high reputation throughout the world for it's products and high standard of craftsmanship and I feel sure that you may rightly assume that this has partly been due to your own contribution and efforts.

We hope that you will retain good health for many years ahead in which to enjoy your own particular hobbies and interests.

The Old 'Uns

In the 1940s and '50s not all the men retired at sixty-five. A lot of men worked into their seventies and some were eighty-year-old when they finished.

Ted Howell

Man and Boy

When William Carney Robinson died in 1957 the *Sunderland Echo* paid tribute to a long serving shipyard worker. When he retired from JL Thompson's just after the Second World War he had been with the firm for over half a century. He started as an apprentice in the 1890s and was a foreman shipwright when he finished working in the yard at the age of seventy.

Right: Former Pickersgill's worker Jack Wilkinson with his retirement cheque. In his younger days Jack was a well-known boxer who fought under the name Clancy. Kenny Downes remembers Jack's retirement party as being a very special occasion with many former boxers turning out that night.

Bartram's workers at Billy Moon's retirement party in the 1970s.

End Of The Day

The Buses

Every evening there would be a fleet of buses which left Fulwell depot going to the shipyards and the other factories in Pallion. On the front of the buses was 'Watson Street' which is where MFI is now.

Stan Fowler

Haversack On Fire

The men at Laing's used to gather at the gates waiting for the end of the shift. I remember one day, about twenty years ago, a man with a haversack full of wood shavings for a rabbit hutch or something was waiting for the buzzer to go. Somebody thought it would be a good laugh to set it alight. It was well ablaze before the startled man was able to put the flames out.

Mickey Stephenson

Toilet Humour

On a night, when the buzzer went, it would be a race to catch the buses. One night I was running for the bus and there was a lad in front of me with a haversack on his back. While he was running his bag burst open and a load of toilet rolls fell out. He had been pinching them from the yard. Everyone had his life for years after that. He never lived it down.

Alf Henderson

The Crowds

When you drove through Pallion at the end of the day there would be thousands of men leaving the shipyards. It was like the crowd leaving a football match. It was tremendous.

Harry Clark

Doxford's in the 1950s. J. Gordon Holmes writing in *The Barbary Coast: The Story Of A Community*, describes the scene when the men left the yards: ' … it was hard luck if you were standing opposite the gate at 12 or 5 o'clock … you'd be knocked down in the mass exodus.'

AROUND THE YARDS

Doxford's … Austin & Pickersgill's … JL Thompson's … Laing's … Bartram's … Short's …

A ship under construction at Doxford's in the 1940s.

Doxford's

William Doxford founded the firm in 1840 and at first built ships at Cox Green before moving to Pallion in 1857. In 1870 he bought the site in Pallion which was to be the company's home for over 100 years. At that time the site consisted of several abandoned shipyards, refuse hills and a lime quarry. The area was levelled and five berths built. William died in 1882 and the yard was run by his four sons, William Theodore, Alfred, Robert and Charles, who in 1891 formed William Doxford and Sons Ltd. The company's capacity was doubled in 1904 when the East Yard was built with three new berths. The extra capacity enabled Doxford's to win the blue riband for shipbuilding with the highest production of any yard in the world in 1904 and 1907.

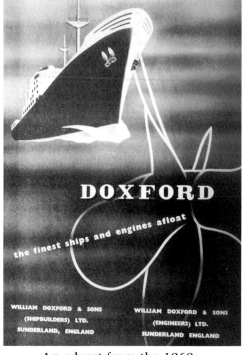

Pallion Lad

The shipyards were a way of life in Sunderland. They always seemed to be there and you always thought they would be there. As a boy growing up in Pallion it was natural for me to go to work in the yards. Living near to Doxford's I was used to the noise from the yard and the mass of men coming to and from work.

Jimmy Mullen

An advert from the 1960s.

Doxford's fitting-out quay.

Above: The three berths at Doxford's East Yard, 1904.

Left: The East Yard in 1904.

Below: The stockyard.

J. Bond, R. Walker and R. Finn at Doxford's in the 1950s.

Doxford's in the late 1940s with a ship on the berth ready for launch.

Stephenson's Rocket

In late 1967 I visited Doxford's shipyard with some other shipbuilding students on an organised trip from West Park College of Further Education. The yard had been completely rebuilt at the turn of the twentieth century and, from what I can remember of our visit in 1967, looked as though there had been little or no investment

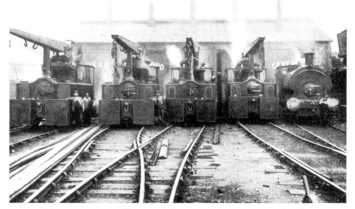

The crane tanks and locomotive at Doxford's.

in over sixty years. The yard was very old and antiquated. The steam powered travelling cranes stand out in my memory. They reminded me of drawings I had seen at school of Stephenson's Rocket. I can remember several of us being showered with water as one of the cranes passed by.

Peter Gibson

The crane tank *Southwick* at Doxford's high level plate yard, 7th March 1970.

The *Southwick* at the end of its working life at Doxford's, 21st February 1971. Other locomotives were the *Pallion, Millfield, Roker* and *Hendon*.

The Building Of A Yard

In 1972 it was decided to demolish the old East Yard at Doxford's and build a state of the art covered shipbuilding hall. Demolition started in late 1972 and was completed in October 1973 when rebuilding work started. The new site was officially opened on 8th April 1976.

An aerial view of the East Yard after demolition in 1973.

Excavation work started on the site on 1st October 1973.

The base of the building hall is completed.

A New Concept

In 1977 the house magazine of the Bank Line shipping company, who had many ships built on the Wear, described the advantages of the new yard at Pallion:

The building of ships remains unhindered by the notorious English climate, and all building operations take place in the most ideal conditions, allowing the most sophisticated of equipment to be used. Painting in a clean dry atmosphere is much more effective in protecting the steelwork, and coatings can be applied to schedule uninterrupted by weather.

As the workers operate in conditions protected by extremes of hot and cold, they are better protected against illness or being laid off due to bad weather conditions. The more congenial working conditions also encourage higher standards of workmanship, and as equipment and services are adjacent to where they are required, time, effort, and cost are reduced particularly in building and outfitting. Lines of communication are also considerably improved due to the improved location of all services ... Pallion is a totally new concept in ship production, which gives new hope that all is not yet lost in Britain as a producer of some of the world's finest ships.

The sheds begin to take shape. At the time of the redevelopment the yard was owned by the Court Shipbuilding Group. In their newsletter, *Courtship*, in September 1973, they proudly described the new yard:

The Pallion yard is gone. The old steel gantries, which so characterised the place and stood out so prominently to anyone looking from across the river, have disappeared without trace. When the gantries were built in 1904, they were the very latest thing in shipbuilding; they enabled the old Doxford yard to achieve its fantastic record of practically a ship a fortnight. Now, 70 years on, the yard will once again be the very latest in shipbuilding ... It will be the most up-to-date yard in Britain, in Europe, probably the world.

The first 'vessel' to be built in the new yard was the 380 tonne Cassian Gate used to keep out the water of the River Wear. Here it is dwarfed by the size of the building hall. The *Cedarbank* was the first ship to be built at the new yard – 'the world's largest covered shipyard'. It was floated out on 26th May 1976.

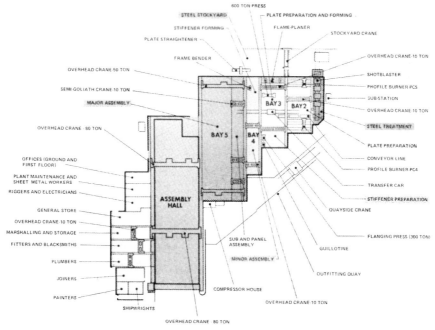

The Pallion layout.

The layout of the yard.

Austin & Pickersgill's

S.P. Austin & Sons, known for building ships for the coal trade, was founded in 1826 on the north side of the Wear and in 1846 moved across the river to a site near Wearmouth Bridge. The yard was famous for its pontoon which opened in 1904 and enabled Austin's to dock ships up to 400 feet in length. Austin's merged with Pickersgill's in 1954 and the yard was closed in 1964.

Austin's pontoon was built by Swan Hunter's at Wallsend and opened on the 28th May 1903. The *Sunderland Daily Echo and Shipping Gazette*, as it was then known, reported that day:

An immense crowd gathered on the Wearmouth Bridge and in the vicinity of the yard to watch the proceedings. The *Brescia*, which is the first Cunarder built on the river, was gaily decked with flags, and lay near to the pontoon. Simply put, the latter contains a number of tanks. Into these the water was allowed to enter, causing it to sink towards the bottom of the river. The *Brescia* was then manoeuvred over the sunken part, partly by means of her winches and partly by hauling of ropes. When in position she was shored to prevent her moving. Internal pumps were then set working to withdraw the water from the tanks. As this was done and the air penetrated the pontoon gradually lifting to the surface, carrying the ship with it, the whole operation of lifting occupied about 45 minutes … The vessel had been placed on the dock in order to have the lower part cleaned and painted, and in a minute after it was clear of the water men were at work scraping it.

S. P. Austin & Son,
—— LIMITED ——

SHIPBUILDERS, SHIP ENGINE
AND BOILER REPAIRERS.

ESTABLISHED 1826.

ON ADMIRALTY LIST.

Pontoon Dock	capable of taking vessels up to 390 feet long.
Graving Dock	do.	do.	to 300	do.
Public Graving Dock	do.	do.	440	do.
Do.	do.	do.	360	do.

Repairing Quays, Pneumatic and Electric Tools. Special Facilities for Quick Dispatch.

Wear Dock Yard, Sunderland.

Telephones—Works; Day & Night, 1254 (5 lines). Telegrams—"Austin, Sunderland."
Manager's Residence, 295. Codes used—Watkin's, Scott's.

Established in 1826, this Company has earned a high reputation as specialists in the building of Colliers, having constructed vessels of this class for most of the leading Collier Owners, and has also had varied experience in the construction of other types of vessels, up to 360ft. in length, always maintaining the highest efficiency.

In the Repairing Department the Company can accommodate vessels up to 390 feet long. its Pontoon and Graving Dock being thoroughly equipped with the necessary plant and machinery to ensure quick dispatch and the highest quality of workmanship; it has always maintained a reputation for giving entire satisfaction.

An advert from the 1920s.

Left: A minesweeper on the pontoon in the 1950s.

William Pickersgill with Messrs Miller, Rawson and Watson started shipbuilding in the North Dock in 1838. Seven years later the firm split, with the former partners moving to Southwick. William Pickersgill emerged as the most prominent shipbuilder and he developed the Southwick site. William was killed in the yard during the construction of the company's second iron ship in 1880. His son, William J. took over the firm and remained there until after the Second World War. During the war Pickersgill's took over the neighbouring John Priestman yard which was a major expansion for the small company.

After Austin's and Pickersgill's merged in 1954, the Southwick yard was redeveloped at a cost of £3 million which took four years to complete. Austin's yard, however, closed in 1964.

A&P became famous for building SD14s (shelterdecker of 14,000 tons dwt) with the first launched from Southwick being the *Nicola* in 1967. The last SD14 launched from Pickie's was the *Sunderland Venture* on 17th November 1983.

A&P News, May 1978.

A Start At Pickie's

You would go down to the 'Market' at half past seven to get a job. You would hear through word of mouth things like, 'They are starting twenty welders at Pickie's tomorrow.' So you would go down to the Market and they would count out the men they wanted and you started the next day. I had heard that Austin & Pickersgill's wanted men so I went down but couldn't find the foreman. I went looking for him on a ship and I got told off. He said, 'You know what time you come looking for work - half past seven or twelve o'clock.' I knew Pickersgill's were starting seven men the following morning and they had already been picked but I still went down the next day. In those days when you started you went to the time officer and got your number. The time keeper said, 'Eight men? – I thought it was only seven - but what's the difference.' So I got a start as well. From that day I stayed at Pickie's for half my working life.

Kenny Downes

The first day of construction of a SD14.

The *Baron Kinnaird* under construction at Austin & Pickersgill's in 1958. She was the second wholly prefabricated ship built at the Southwick yard and was said at the time to be the most advanced vessel ever built by the company. Her launch was delayed for a month because there was no fitting-out berth for the ship. At that time Austin & Pickersgill's were building a new quay as part of a major expansion programme.

Shipwrights from Pickersgill's take a break from working on a minesweeper in the 1950s.

Redevelopment at Pickersgill's in the 1950s showing a new fitting-out quay under construction.

Ahead Of The Rest

Austin & Pickersgill's were, in most things, years ahead of other yards in wages and conditions. When we became part of British Shipbuilders, Pickersgill's ceased to be an individual yard and became part of this larger group. We would then go to meetings with other yards all around the country. They would talk about new ideas which they wanted to introduce but we were often already doing it. Our wage structure was way ahead of everybody else. When we came into British Shipbuilders all the other yards had to catch up to our wage structure.

Kenny Downes

Right: The fitting-out quay in 1991 after Austin & Pickersgill's had closed. In the background, demolition of the yard has started.

Shipyard manager, Tommy Bell (left) and foreman burner, George Gray in the
construction hall at Austin & Pickersgill's in the early 1980s. Tommy Bell
recalled how he enjoyed his time at Pickersgill's even though there were a lot
of hard times. 'Many a day and night I spent there. For the last ship I
completed, I slept the last two nights on board. I was never off the ship for
four days.'

Steel plates being brought into Austin & Pickersgill's, 22nd August 1983.

The *Fayrouz IV* at Pickersgill's fitting-out quay in May 1984.

The retirement evening for former Austin & Pickersgill's worker, John Bryce at
Southwick Club. John is in the centre of the picture with his wife. Also on
stage are Tom Lowden, head foreman welder at Pickie's and shop stewards:
Kenny Downes, Alan Clarke and Harry Scott.

JL Thompson's

Robert Thompson was the first member of this well-known shipbuilding family to work on the Wear and he built ships at several sites during the mid-nineteenth century. In 1846, Robert and his three sons started work at North Sands and in eleven weeks, working with four other men, they built their first ship. Over the next few years the yard quickly developed. Robert died in 1860 and the following year only one son remained with the company – Joseph Lowes. In 1875 Joseph L. Thompson retired and his three sons took over. The company continued for the next 100 years and some of the biggest ships on the Wear were built at the yard. After the launch of the *Badagry Palm* in 1979 the yard was mothballed. The Manor Quay continued to be used for outfitting by Doxford's and Laing's. The North Sands yard was re-opened in 1986 to build a massive crane ship, the *Challenger*. However, the firm who ordered the ship went into receivership and the vessel was laid up in the river for many months before a new buyer was found. The site of JL Thompson's has now been transformed with the University of Sunderland taking over most of the land for its St Peter's Campus.

Right: An advert from the 1920s.

Joseph L. Thompson and Sons, Ltd.,

NORTH SANDS
Shipbuilding Yard
——and——
MANOR QUAY
Repairing Works,
SUNDERLAND.

ESTABLISHED 1846.

Builders and Repairers of all types of Passenger vessels, Merchant vessels, Bulk Oil tankers, and Refrigerated vessels.

STEAM OR MOTOR DRIVEN.

HIGH CLASS WORK.

Graving Docks:
500 ft., 441 ft., and 356 ft. long.
Quay at Works: 750 ft. long.

TELEGRAMS: "THOMSONIAN, SUNDERLAND."
TELEPHONE NOS., 1242 & 1243.

The bulk carrier *Borgsten* under construction at JL Thompson's North Sands yard in the early 1960s.

JL Thompson's North Sands yard, 1946.

The Manor Quay, 1946.

Keep Out Of The Yards

I left school in July 1966 and in September I started work as an apprentice shipbuilder at JL Thompson's. I had just turned fifteen and the shipyard was a culture shock after experiencing the relative cosiness of the classroom. About forty-four apprentices started work at JL's (the big yard) that year and during an introductory tour of the yard an old man shouted to us – 'Keep out of the yards.' It was something my dad had also said to me. I didn't really understand what they meant, but I was soon to find out.

My first nine months as an apprentice shipbuilder were spent at college and interspersed with short periods in the shipyard. My first experience of a shipyard in winter was at JL's over Christmas 1966 when the college closed for two weeks. Probably most of my peers weren't prepared for conditions in the yard. I certainly wasn't. Overalls and protective footwear were not supplied in those days and I turned up for work in my college clothes. Mainly because of naivety and because I didn't have any work clothes.

THE AMALGAMATED SOCIETY OF BOILERMAKERS, SHIPWRIGHTS BLACKSMITHS AND STRUCTURAL WORKERS OF GREAT BRITAIN & IRELAND (BOILERMAKERS SECTION)

BRANCH *S.LAND 7*
LODGE No. *APP 46*

BRO. *P.S. GIBSON*
Address *61 Shakespeare St*
Southwick

Registered No. ....
Branch of Trade *SC*
Benefit Section *APP*

J. McArdle President
J. Meekins Secretary
13 Faber Rd Address
Southwick

Peter Gibson's first union card.

With three other apprentices, I was sent to work with some welders on what was known as the 'top gantry'. It was bitterly cold. During bait time we crowded around the fire (what appeared to be a large old paint tin with holes burnt in it which gave out a glowing warmth) to the side of the gantry. I hadn't been exposed to long periods of intense cold like this before and the cold steel and drafts made matters worse. A tacker gave us some tea with rum in it to warm us up. The other apprentices and I were tempted back to the warmth of the fire after bait time. A foreman welder appeared on the scene while we were thawing out. He ordered us back on to our jobs, but before we could move he kicked over the fire. Ashes, sparks and burning wood scattered everywhere. The gaffer then looked on to the gantry as if wanting to see if any of the welders had anything to say. Heads disappeared into screens. I remember being surprised by his violent action. I hadn't seen anything like it before from a man. The harsh weather, inadequate clothing, the dark mornings, the tiredness brought on by long hours and the lack of shipyard sense all added up to a pretty miserable initiation into the yards. I felt relieved to go back to college after the Christmas period.

I was better prepared for my second spell at JL's at Easter 1967. My dad gave me a coat which a mate at work had given him. It sticks in my memory because of its comparison to the radical 1960s fashions of the time. The large dress coat was grey with prominent chalk stripes, double breasted and padded shoulders. It was like something from a gangster movie. Florrie, my mother-in-law, had knitted me a woollen hat, and I was surprised how much heat a scarf could keep in. I bought a pair of steel toe-capped boots from the shipyard store. The five shillings which were docked from my wages until they were paid for put a big hole in my weekly take home pay.

Peter Gibson

The North Sands yard with a P&O tanker under construction in the 1950s.

One of the last big ships goes down the slipway at JL Thompson's.

Laing's

Philip Laing started building ships at Deptford in 1818 and his son, James, was born in the shipyard in 1823. James took over the yard when he was twenty and quickly developed the company.

The Torrens was launched from Laing's in 1875 and it went on to become one of the most famous ships ever built in Sunderland. The novelist Joseph Conrad sailed on the ship as second mate and he described it as, 'A ship of brilliant qualities'.

In 1898 the company's name changed to Sir James Laing and Sons after James was knighted the year before. Sir James died in 1907 and two years later, when the yard had financial problems, Sir James Marr was appointed to the board and became Chairman in 1912. Marr was one of the most influential figures in Sunderland shipbuilding and created the link between Thompson's, Laing's and Sunderland Forge.

Sir James Laing
and Sons, Ltd.,

DEPTFORD YARD,
SUNDERLAND.

BUILDERS
——— OF ———

High-Class Cargo, Passenger, and Oil Carrying Vessels.

———

Dock Owners.

———

Brass & Iron Founders, and Coppersmiths.

———

ON ADMIRALTY LIST.

———

Telegrams :   Telephones :
"Laing, Sunderland."   1490, 1491, 1492.

Three men at Laing's, *circa* 1950. Left to right: Ronnie Drummond, John Sweeney, Albert Owens.

An advert from the 1920s.

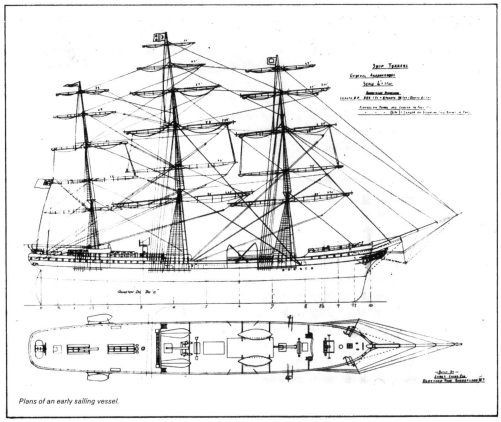

Plans of an early sailing vessel.

Plans for the most famous ship ever built on the Wear – *The Torrens* –
launched from Laing's in 1875.

Laing's in the late 1940s.

The *Troutbank*

The construction of the *Troutbank* - launched from Laing's, 26th April 1979.

Bartram's

George Bartram started building ships at Hylton in 1837. The business moved to the South Dock in 1871 and was known as Bartram and Haswell – after its owners R.A. Bartram (George's son) and George Haswell. In 1889 Haswell retired and the remaining partner was joined by his two sons to form Bartram & Sons Ltd.

The firm was unique in that it launched ships direct into the North Sea. During the Second World War it also had the distinction of employing the first woman welder to join the Boilermaker's Society, Mrs Collard.

Bartram's was taken over by Austin & Pickersgill's and the two yards started building SD14s in 1967. In 1978 the yard closed and the workforce moved to Pickersgill's.

An advert from the 1950s.

A SD14 under construction at Bartram's.

The Move To Pickersgill's

Few of the Bartram's lads could settle at Pickersgill's when the two yards were merged. Even though the conditions were much better – Pickersgill's had just built a new complex while working conditions in Bartram's were poor - it didn't make any difference. We were strangers at Pickersgill's and most of the men took redundancy as soon as they could. We thought we would all move into the new complex they had just built at Pickersgill's but when we got there we were spread out through the yard. We just couldn't gel. I only stayed a couple of years. I had even served my time at Pickersgill's but I still couldn't settle.

Ted Howell

Welders in the Assembly Shop at Bartram's in the 1950s.

The *Arraiolos* being towed into the South Dock for fitting-out after being launched from Bartram's on 22nd April 1948. The ship was one of six Portuguese vessels in the yard at that time – three were on the berths and three were fitting-out in the South Dock. The yard, like many on the Wear at that time, was enjoying a boom period and when one ship was launched there was another to start work on. The *Arraiolos* was launched on the Thursday and the keel of its sister ship was laid in the vacant berth on the Monday.

The *Rovuma*, launched into the sea from Bartram's, July 1946. The launch was filmed and shown at the Havelock Cinema, on the corner of High Street and Fawcett Street, a few months later.

Bartram's, February 1948.

Short's

This family firm was founded by George Short in 1850 and Short's sons, grandsons and great grandsons worked in the yard. Short's moved to Pallion in 1869 and it became known as the 'local' yard as the company built more ships for local owners than any other on the Wear. Short's closed with the loss of 300 jobs in 1964 when the firm was unwilling to redevelop the yard to build bigger ships. The yard was demolished with Bartram's taking over the fitting-out quay which was still in use by Austin & Pickersgill's in the 1980s.

Right: An advert from the 1950s.

Below: The *Vigrafjord* being towed under Wearmouth Bridge. The ship was launched from Short's on 4th April 1955.

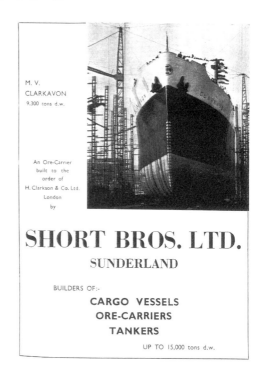

M. V.
CLARKAVON
9,300 tons d.w.

An Ore-Carrier
built to the
order of
H. Clarkson & Co. Ltd.
London
by

SHORT BROS. LTD.
SUNDERLAND

BUILDERS OF:-

CARGO VESSELS
ORE-CARRIERS
TANKERS

UP TO 15,000 tons d.w.

The bulk carrier *World Explorer* launched from Short's at 4 am on 25th October 1962. It was the first launch from Short's in darkness for forty years. The launch had twice been postponed due to gales and if the tide had not risen high enough on this day there would have a been a delay of another month before conditions were right. The men worked by arc light and moonlight. During the First World War Short's launched the *War Seagull* by the light from tallow candles.

A Well Made Ship

I thought Short's built some of the best ships on the Wear. Perhaps being a small yard with not a big workforce they could spend a little extra time on each ship. The likes of Doxford's and Pickie's seemed to churn out ships one after the other.

Jimmy Taylor

Wages In A Tin

At Short's we used to get our wages in a little tin. Sometimes people would quickly empty out the tin and give it back not realising the notes were still in it. Many a time I went back to get the rest of my money – I had only emptied out the coppers.

Ted Howell

SECTION THREE

EVERY LAUNCH WAS SPECIAL

Knocking Out The Last Chock … The Rattle Of The Chains … A Broadside Launch … A Launch Time Drink … SD14s … The Last Launch At Laing's …

The launch of the *Colima*, from Laing's, 30th July 1984. In the foreground is the tug *Ironsider*.

A launch from Doxford's.

Great Times

Every launch was special. There was a real sense of achievement that you had built something. The ship had grown from nothing. You could say there's another good job done.

Tommy Bell

Times Of Cheer

Everyone in the yard would turn out to see the launches. They would all come out of the offices – draughtsmen, collar and tie men. All the dust would fly up with the chains and the ship would float into the water and everyone would cheer. My Uncle Jack would knock out the last chock to launch the ship.

Alf Henderson

On arriving in Pallion, to work in Sunderland, 'the largest shipbuilding town in the world', I was amazed to see how narrow the River Wear looked at Pallion … It seemed hardly credible that the fine ships for which Sunderland is famous, could be launched into such a small space. Of course, I did not then understand the very skilful use that is made of drag-chains when a ship is launched here – always at high tide – after the most careful calculations. Nor did one at once visualise the way in which the utmost use is made of bends in the river, to enable ships to be launched up or down into the mid-stream of the river.

C.H.C. Hopkins
Pallion: Church and People in a Shipyard Parish (1954)

High Times

Launches were a real treat for us young kids as all the families in Deptford used to gather down at the river. We waited for the new ship to be let loose and listened for the rattle of the chains as the ship slid down the ramp. The cheers as the ship hit the water still make me feel on a high. I married a shipyard worker and I used to obtain a pass which allowed me and my little boy Neil into Doxford's to watch new ships being launched.

Audrey Henderson

Under Steam

Sometimes someone would light a bag in the funnel as a ship was launched and the ship would go down the berth with smoke coming out of the funnel as if it was under steam.

Tommy Bell

Fill The Bar

After a launch at JL Thompson's we used to go straight into the Marquis of Lorne for a pint. The night before one launch we were having a drink in the Marquis and the landlord said he would have the drinks lined up on the bar ready for us the next day. After the ship was sent down the slipway the lads arranged to meet in the Vulcan instead. As we were passing we looked in the window of the Marquis to see sixty or seventy pints lined up on the bar. The landlord waved us in but to his amazement we went next door to the Vulcan.

Billy Dent

Shipwrights from Doxford's in the 1950s. Jack Henderson is second from the left. His nephew Alf remembers the times when Jack would knock away the last chock to send the ships on their way into the river.

HMS *Kedleston*, launched from Pickersgill's on the 21st December 1953, was the first Naval ship built on the Wear since the Second World War. The minesweeper was built of aluminium and wood so as to be non-magnetic. Mr F.W. Hopper, Managing Director of Pickersgill's said at the launch, 'We feel this ship is being built for peace and goodwill to ships on the seas – merchant ships. We trust the time will not come when this vessel has to be used.'

The launch of the tanker *British Cavalier* from JL Thompson's on 19th June 1962. At the time it was the biggest ship built on the Wear and crowds flocked to the river banks to see the launch. So great was the crowd that after the launch people moving away from the river caused traffic jams in the town centre.

Welsh Trader

The *Welsh Trader* was the first prefabricated ship built at Pickersgill's. It was built through trial and error over thirteen months, from laying the keel to the launch. It was partly riveted and partly welded. We tried different methods of fabricating parts of the ship. It was a good ship when it was finished – and so it should have been with all that work.

Tommy Bell

Right: The *Welsh Trader*, launched 28th June 1954. Mr F.W. Hopper, Managing Director of Pickersgill's, said after the launch that his workers were underrated: 'The British workmen should be given a pat on the back more often. If he gets a really hard, tough job he sets about it with a will. He doesn't like to be pampered and made a fuss of; what he wants is really good interesting hard work and he enjoys it. I think we are spoiling him by giving him silly jobs. What he likes is some big object and he gets on with the job.'

Left to right: Tommy Bell, head foreman shipwright, Alec Hiddlestone shed production manager, Fred Rogers berth manager, at Pickersgill's, *circa* 1970.

SD 14s

The SD14 was a famous Sunderland export and one of the most successful designs of its day. In the early 1960s Austin & Pickersgill's realised that the Liberty ships – built during the Second World War – would be twenty years old by 1965. They knew replacements would be needed and after much research came up with the design of the SD14. The first ships were built by Austin & Pickersgill's and Bartram's in 1967. The design was used by shipbuilders throughout the world and by 1982 the 200th SD14 had been launched in Brazil.

Sunderland Venture

The last SD14 I worked on was the *Sunderland Venture*. It was built for a Hong Kong owner. He had studied at Sunderland Polytechnic and had done some practical work at Austin and Pickersgill's. The town was his second home and so when he had his own company he decided to have a ship built at Sunderland.

Tommy Bell

Right: An advert from the 1970s.

FOURTH SERIES

Announcing –

A NEW, IMPROVED version of the most widely accepted post-war general cargo vessel :—

- Modified hull form
- Lower fuel consumption
- Improved bale stowage
- Heavier cargo gear
- Rationalised accommodation
- Redesigned navigating bridge
- New Sulzer 'M' type main engine
- Enhanced specification

AUSTIN & PICKERSGILL
SUNDERLAND

The SD14 *Syrie*, launched from Austin & Pickersgill's, 14th February 1968.

The Bank Line

The Bank Line, whose parent company was Andrew Weir, had a long association with Sunderland shipbuilding. The company's first ship built on the Wear was the *Gifford*, launched from Doxford's in 1913. In the following sixty years over fifty Bank Line ships were built in the town.

Right: Mrs J.G. Young and Mr J.P. Gilfillan, Chairman and Managing Director of Sunderland Shipbuilders, after the naming of the Bank Line company's *Streambank* on 7th March 1977. Mrs Young, wife of one of the directors of the London shipping company, had named the ship at Greenwell's Quay. The *Streambank* was the third ship completed at the new Pallion Yard.

The *Nessbank* under construction at Doxford's in the 1970s.

The *Murree*

A tradition at Pickersgill's was for two men and their wives to be invited to launch parties. They were often men due to retire. On one occasion, Tom Richardson and his wife Edith were invited to the launch of the *Murree*.

DINNER

preceding the launch of

m.v. 'MURREE'

for Pakistan National Shipping Corporation

The Royal Station Hotel, Newcastle upon Tyne
Thursday 4th December 1980

Built by
Austin & Pickersgill Limited
Southwick Shipyard, Sunderland

The cover of the menu for the dinner celebrating the launch of the *Murree*. The ship, the first SD18, was built for the Pakistan National Shipping Corporation and was named after a summer resort in Pakistan.

The launch of the *Murree*, 5th December 1980.

Tom Richardson (centre) with his wife Edith chat to a director of Austin & Pickersgill's at the dinner for the launch of the *Murree*.

The launch of the *Baron Ardrossan* at Pickersgill's on 5th April 1954. The name of the ship was a 500-year-old title held by the Earl of Eglington. The ship was owned by the Glasgow company H. Hogarth & Sons, who named all their ships after Scottish barons – it was their fifth vessel with this name. The ship was launched by Mrs J. MacLeod the wife of one of the company's directors. After the launch her husband praised Sunderland craftsmanship, '… a Pickersgill-built ship meant a good ship and that the workmanship would be perfect. The name Pickersgill was the hallmark … We look forward to chartering the *Baron Ardrossan*. With such a fine ship we shall play havoc with our competitors.'

Opposite page: The *Sir Johnstone Wright*, launched from Pickersgill's on 18th August 1955. She was a collier built for the Central Electricity Authority and named after its former Chairman. At one time colliers were a common sight off the North East coast carrying coal from the region's pits to the South.

The *Sir Johnstone Wright* was the first of three ships launched in Sunderland in five days. The following day JL Thompson's launched the *Troutpool* with Bartram's launching the *Despina C* three days later. The *Despina C* was named after Despina Cosmas whose father was the Managing Director of the ship's owners. Despina had travelled from San Francisco with her family to break the traditional bottle of champagne against the bows of the ship. After the launch she said, 'I am nine tomorrow and the best birthday present of all is being allowed to sponsor this vessel.'

A sailor gang from Pickersgill's on board a ship on trial in the early 1960s.

Above: The *Riverbank* being towed out of Doxford's in 1977. The ship was the 50th Bank Line ship built in Sunderland. On the day she was named, Lord Inverforth, Chairman of the shipping company, opened a garden at Doxford's to be used by the workers. The garden had been paid for by the Bank Line and at its opening Lord Inverforth said, 'This garden is still immature but we hope it will flourish as Pallion is flourishing.' On the same day he announced that a new order for six ships, worth £50 million, would be built at Pallion and Deptford.

A more traditional launch from Doxford's. The launch of the *Stonegate,* on 10th November 1927, was the first at the yard in three years.

A broadside launch from Robert Thompson's yard.

The *Barbara* at Laing's fitting-out quay in 1962 with Wearmouth Colliery in the background. The ship was built for a Swedish owner and it is the custom in that country to keep the name of the vessel a secret until it is launched. When the *Barbara* was launched from Laing's, on 4th May 1962, the name was covered up and as the ship went down the slipway a yellow drape was removed to reveal her name.

The launch of the *Mitla* on 3 May 1985. It was to be last ship built at Laing's. The site is now used by the crane company, Liebherr who employ many former shipyard workers.

The *Mitla*

In 1985, as part of the local studies curriculum, I took a class from Redby Junior School to Laing's to watch the launch of the *Mitla*. We all went with great anticipation of a memorable spectacle and weren't disappointed. To see, close up, a brand new ship seemingly perfectly balanced on its wooden chocks certainly took the breath away. I remember the arrival of the launch party and the extravagant fur coats and expensive jewellery adorning the wives of the shipowners. As the final chock was hammered away and the champagne duly delivered, the accompanying cheers of the workers and spectators were quickly drowned out by the roar of the drag chains. Balloons and coloured smoke were released from the ship as it slid gracefully into the water. I asked the worker who had hammered away the final white painted chock if I could take it as a souvenir. I carried it back to school where it was proudly displayed alongside the children's accounts of the day. At the end of term I took home this precious piece of Sunderland shipbuilding history wondering what to do with it. My wife, Margaret, solved the problem. She stuck it in the shed and waited until I had forgotten all about it before discretely disposing of it during a Spring clean. Another piece of Sunderland's heritage lost forever!

Phil Curtis

Special Days

With my family living near Pickie's I had watched their launches since I was a young girl – I can still hear the rattle of the chains. They were special days for local people and its a shame that our kids will never see sights like that.

Doris Downes

A DANGEROUS PLACE

*The Noise Just Hit You … Welder's Lung … Asbestos … An
Apprentice's Accident … The Blood Yards … Family Tragedy …*

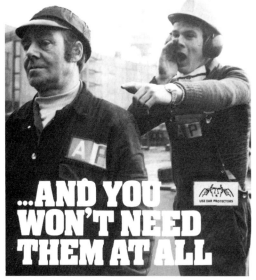

A safety advert from the *A&P News*, March 1978.

No Stopping

You had to be tough to work in the yards in my day. If you got a cut you just sucked the wound and got on with your work.

Tom Richardson

The Cold Shift

It used to be freezing down at Bartram's with the wind coming off the sea. On nightshift I would wear two coats, a balaclava and a scarf to work.

Tommy Fairley

Always Cold And Wet

You always seemed to be cold and wet even in the summer. It might have been a warm day but you would still be working on a steel plate which was cold. That's why so many men suffer from arthritis.

Ted Howell

Candles In The Yards

When I started at Laing's in 1943 we had to use candles when we were working on the double bottoms of the ships. There were no tea breaks. You had to have a cuppa when no-one was watching. The toilets were never cleaned and there was never any hand basins.

John Humphreys

In The Dark

When you walked into the blacksmith's shop in the 1940s and '50s you couldn't see a thing for smoke. You could hardly see the fires it was so bad. Blazing fires looked like fag ends in the darkness. It would take you half an hour before your eyes adjusted to the light and by then you were covered in dust.

Ted Howell

Austin's shipyard, winter 1955. Although this scene shows the worst side of the weather, Austin's normally had better conditions at launch time. For twenty years every launch from the yard took place in fine weather.

Nightshift at JL Thompson's, October 1951.

Asbestos

The welding rods had asbestos wrapped around them. The dangers of asbestos are known now but at that time it was never thought about. Although even as early as the 1930s they were looking into the safety of asbestos and some people probably knew of the dangers. But we didn't know of course and we were the ones exposed to it.

Harry Gibson

Radiation

At Doxford's in the early 1980s an X-Ray machine was being used to check some welding. Because of the danger of radiation it was done at bait time with the area cordoned off with tape. As the job was being X-Rayed, a bloke walked straight though the cordon. Someone shouted, 'Watch out. Radiation!' The bloke just pulled his donkey jacket over his head.

Steve James

The Noise

The noise was terrible in the shipyards. These doctors who tell us we aren't deaf through working in the yards couldn't have spent a day there. We had to put up with the noise from the squads of riveters, caulkers and drillers every day all day.

Bob Simpson

It Just Hit You

Going into Laing's on my first day in 1959 was awesome. There was still a lot of riveting at that time and when I first walked into the yard the noise just hit you. You didn't have ear protection in those days so you did what you could with a couple of pieces of cotton wool. But some people who saw you with cotton wool in your ears thought you were soft.

Kenny Downes

Eye Strain

I was always at the Eye Infirmary. I was a plater and if I helped a burner I often got something in my eye. I was always getting flashes from the welders.

Alf Henderson

Little Protection

I was a welder and started my apprenticeship at Bartram's in 1952. The apprentices never wore much protective clothing apart from gloves. We weren't allowed welding capes or sleeves. It was only after 1979 that they got the proper extraction system to take away the fumes from welding. You were working in a confined space with very little extraction. You did have what was called a windy pipe extraction which did take some of the fumes away but that was all we had.

John Banks

My First Flash

I still remember my first flash, or arc-eye as it was also known, when I was welding in Thompson's Palmer's Hill Shed in 1967 when I was fifteen. We had been warned on many occasions to shield our eyes from welding rays but that was difficult as there were welders and tackers striking up all around. I had been instructed on the cause and symptoms of a flash. The welding rays burn a layer of skin in the eye. Nothing happens at the time, but several hours later and usually during the night it feels as though hot sand was being poured into your eyes which fill up with water and extreme soreness is experienced. I had several flashes during my time in the yards, but my first flash was the worst. Wearing safety glasses prevented a flash but we had to buy them in those days from the shipyard store at the Manor Quay.

Peter Gibson

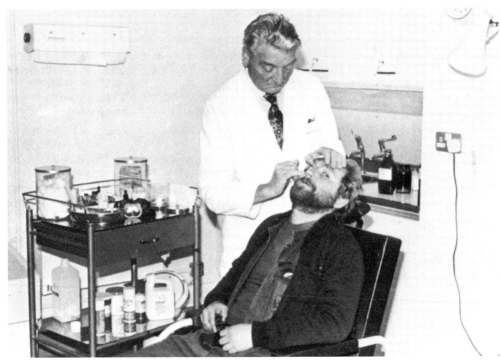

Platers helper, Alan Jackson has his eye examined by Cyril Richardson at Austin & Pickersgill's in 1982.

The Fumes

When you looked into a tank where three or four welders were working you could hardly see the lights of the welding arcs because it was that thick with fumes. If any of the men who worked in those conditions has good health now they have been very lucky.

Bob Simpson

Welder's Lung

The only extraction you really had was wind. Through breathing all those fumes I've got welder's lung. I've also got arthritis in the hands and legs through working in terrible conditions. Most men who worked in those conditions have health problems. Men I know in their seventies can't catch their breath and that's because of what they had to put up with from working in the yards.

Ronnie Stubbs

We All Suffer

We all seem to have welder's lung, vibration white finger or poor eyesight. All the shipyard men suffer from something.

Ted Howell

Left: Arthur Dykes at Laing's, *circa* 1960. Like many former shipyard men, Arthur now suffers from arthritis from the working conditions he was forced to endure. This photograph illustrates the precarious positions men often had to work in. He is twenty feet off the ground and has no safety rail.

Ambulances In The Yard

I don't think a day went by when an ambulance wasn't at JL Thompson's. We had more deaths than I wish to remember in our yard. The majority of these came from falls from staging. Losing fingers was also a common occurrence with men often getting their hands caught between metal plates.

Billy Dent

Right: Billy Dent – who started at JL Thompson's in 1956 and served his apprenticeship as a welder. Billy is a keen collector of shipyard memorabilia and old postcards of Sunderland. In 1997 part of his postcard collection was published in the book *Something For You From Sunderland.*

The Blood Yards

They used to call Doxford's and JL Thompson's the 'blood yards' because they had so many accidents. Bartram's, where I worked for many years, was a much safer yard.

Ted Howell

Funerals

Over the years, funerals of welders I worked with at Austin & Pickersgill's have become more and more frequent. Many of these were not old men, but men only in their fifties or touching sixty.

Stu McSween

A Dying Breed

Every time you pick up the newspaper you seem to read of the deaths of shipyard men. They don't seem to last very long after they retire – the boilermakers in particular. I had never been to the crematorium in my life until I became a shop steward and then I was going four or five times a year – every year. And that was just the men I was acquainted with or part of the welding department at Austin & Pickersgill's.

Kenny Downes

JL Thompson's, *circa* 1956. Billy Dent, remembers Thompson's as a hazardous workplace with ambulances regularly coming into the yard.

A Near Miss

For many years it wasn't uncommon to see something fall or collapse. There was one time when I was sitting on a tank top and they were berthing a big girder above me. I had my welding screen on and so couldn't see much around me. I just felt some muck on the back of my neck and took off my screen and stood up. As I looked up, down came the girder and smashed into the wooden box I had been sitting on. The box was smashed and so was my welding screen. There was a lad called Freddie Smith who saw it happen and he went home bad.

Kenny Downes

Kenny Downes receives his prize for winning the *A&P News* quiz from Ernie Howey.

Savage Amusement

I more than doubled my take home pay when I began working at the successful Austin and Pickersgill's yard on nightshift in March 1976. There is one particular job on the SD14s which stands out in my memory – welding the join-up in the engine room double bottom sump. The sump was like a tunnel divided into four compartments – two either side of the centre line. Each compartment was about 2' 6" high and welding the join-up was a real pain. To do the job, tall welders were forced to lie down, whereas being a smaller man I could cope with this type of job by sitting in the join-up space cross-legged and hunched up.

On one occasion, while welding the overhead sealing, a globule of molten metal penetrated my pig skin jacket through a gap between the press studs caused by my cramped posture. The molten metal burnt through my clothing to my chest and continued down through the gap between my stomach and jeans, again caused by my cramped position. It then burnt through my underpants and I dropped everything and cupped my hands against the lower part of my stomach to stop it going further down. It all happened in an instant but I can still remember the smell of singeing hair until the metal cooled down. My skin was burnt slightly but at least I prevented an embarrassing visit to the nurse for treatment.

On another occasion I was welding a pad for a fitter's pipe in the sump. Suddenly there was a loud bang from an explosion. With the benefit of hindsight the combined echo from my head screen, the confined space and the tunnel had grossly exaggerated the 'explosion'. The shock and the claustrophobic atmosphere caused me to make a quick exit from the sump as I scrambled through the spaces and shot out the end almost hitting my mate with my boots until I came to rest breathing heavily. I had suspected that gas was present from an adjoining tank where I knew a burner was working. However, the bang was actually caused by a small patch of oil igniting behind the pad I was welding. No doubt I was the target for some mickey taking for the rest of the day after the incident. It was savage amusement welding in the sump, particularly in hot weather.

Peter Gibson

Welders at Pickersgill's brave the cold in 1986. Left to right: Dave Aldridge, Jim Alderson, Peter Gibson, Gordon Snow.

Men at Doxford's wearing the typical working clothes of the 1950s. In those days flat caps were more common than safety helmets.

Dangerous Journey

There was a fitter at Laing's who used to come to work on his motorbike. He used to drive through the yard and park it outside the fitters' shop. One winter morning he was riding in when he hit a patch of ice and went straight into the river. He got out but I'm not sure what happened to his bike.

Bob Palmer

The Rescuer

One ship was at the quayside getting finished when somebody shouted, 'Man over board.' A shipwright dived straight into the water to save him – he didn't even look over. He got a medal for that.

Bob Simpson

Danger Above

We did not wear safety hats at Laing's until the 1960s. Before then there were more split heads than enough. Nuts and bolts were always falling off staging. One day I was working below some riveters when a piece of metal fell on my head and I had to go to the medical centre. The wound did not need stitching and I was patched up and went back to work. Half an hour later exactly the same thing happened. You couldn't wait until the riveters had finished above you and flat caps were no protection.

Arthur Dykes

Third Time
Lucky

I worked for fourteen years at Doxford's until I had three near misses with accidents. Each time I was lucky – I felt I could have been killed by any of the accidents. I left as soon as I could and got a job in a factory.

Tom Richardson

A New Suit

It was Boxing Day during the war and I was the only apprentice working that day. At that time Pickersgill's had derricks and not cranes. The derricks were lifting a fresh water tank that went between the decks. The tank was for a ship which was bigger than the ones we normally built so consequently the tank was bigger than normal. The tank was too heavy for the derrick and it came crashing down. The lad in the derrick was Bob Wake and he went through one of the sheds and he was hanging by his finger tips. Everyone was dashing around looking for a ladder to get him down. Eventually we got him down but he must have been hanging there for about twenty minutes. William Pickersgill came into the yard when it happened and he said to Bob, 'Are you all right?'

'I am apart from me clothes', Bob said. All his clothes were in rags from coming through the roof.

Pickersgill said, 'I'll bring you a new suit in tomorrow.'

And he did. It was a good suit and Bob said, 'I'm not wearing this for work.' He used to walk around the town with it on.

Tommy Bell

Knockout Cricket

During the 1950s in the summer we used to play cricket at breaktime at Laing's. The pitch was the concrete yard, the bat was made in the joiners' shop and the ball was welder's tape packed solid. One day the batsman hit this hard ball straight at a bloke watching the game. It hit him smack in the forehead and knocked him out cold. There was silence and for a moment we thought he was dead. After a couple of minutes he came round and we got on with the game with the spectators moving to safer positions.

Bob Palmer

The heavy industrial scene of a Sunderland shipyard – Doxford's in the 1950s.

Left: The *Richard de Larrinaga* under construction at Pickersgill's in the 1950s – a time before strict safety regulations.

Nasty Fall

A red-leader at Laing's was climbing a ladder between decks when he caught his foot in the handle of his paint tin. He fell on the tank top, landing on his hands and knees. The bones in his wrists were sticking out through his skin and he climbed back up the ladder in a state of shock. When he got to the top he said to a bloke, 'Give me a fag.' He was then taken off to hospital.

Pearce Gibson

One In The Face

I had a few accidents during my time at Pickie's. One day I was beside a load being lifted by a crane when the sling sprung loose. It hit me in the face and I bit a piece of my tongue off. There was blood all over and I was taken to hospital for treatment.

Another time, during a gale, part of the roof of the shed was blown off. A few days later I was climbing a wet ladder to my crane when I slipped. I fell and hurt my back and was off work a month.

Derek Laidler

An Apprentice's Accident

I was only seventeen when I was working with a plater in the fabrication shed on a guillotine that chopped the plates. It had a little hand crane which you worked yourself. Being an apprentice, I was over the moon to work it. The plater I was working with was talking to someone and while I was just waiting for him I didn't realise I had my finger on the button of the crane. The sling was going up and it caught under the guillotine. It snapped and hit me full in the face. My nose broke, I had two black eyes and all my hair had to be shaved off. I was in a right state. I've still got the scar nearly forty years later.

Alf Henderson

Death Of A Shipwright

A shipwright was once killed when a rudder fell and crushed him. One of the men working nearby was first there and he tried to lift up the rudder. It was twenty ton but he still tried to lift it off the man. But he was killed outright.

Bob Simpson

A Launch Accident

I worked at Laing's and one day we were watching the launch of the *Caltex Tanganyika* from Doxford's in 1951. Something went wrong with the launch and a number of shipwrights were hurt by the drag chains and flying timber. One man was killed. The lady who launched the ship was tearing strips of her dress to use as bandages for the men who were hurt. After that disaster the foreman shipwright at Laing's would only allow two men under the ship at the time of a launch.

Ed MacKenzie

The scene just after a launch at Pickersgill's, *circa* 1950. It shows the dangerous position men were in at launch time. In the centre of the picture is Tommy Dobson, foreman shipwright.

Family Tragedy

I had two brothers killed in the yards. Both had served in the army through the war. One was killed by a twenty foot plank that fell and the other slipped and hit the back of his head.

Bob Simpson

Carry On Working

I was working that Sunday when seven men were killed in Doxford's when there was an explosion. Work didn't completely stop in the yard and we carried on working. When I was working at Greenwell's we stopped work for the day when there was an accident. But often in the yards you carried on working.

Phil Sydney

Doxford's Tragedy

On Sunday 30th October 1966 an explosion on the Toronto City at Doxford's killed seven men. The Times described the tragedy on its front page:

Seven men died this afternoon after an explosion in the propeller shaft tunnel of a new ship being fitted-out at the Sunderland Shipyard of William Doxford & Sons. They were working on board the 10,000-ton cargo motor ship *Toronto Star* which was due to be delivered to the Bibby Line of Liverpool next month.

After the alarm had been given by others working on the vessel, firemen and shipyard men worked side by side for three hours to bring out the bodies.

The firemen, wearing breathing apparatus, fought the fire which followed the explosion 36 ft below decks and brought it under control in about 20 minutes. A hole was cut in the tank top to make access to the propeller shaft tunnel easier and to clear dense smoke as the firemen made their way 50 ft along the tunnel to the seat of the fire.

The Sunderland Chief Fire Officer, Mr Robert Cooper, said, 'At first the men were working in dense smoke on their hands and knees, but as conditions improved they were able to stand up.'

He said one man escaped the fire and another got halfway out of the escape hatch but died in the attempt. The other six dead men were all trapped in the tunnel. Mr Cooper went on, 'We had two jets at work, one down the escape hatch and another from the forward end where the propeller shaft meets the engine room. We got three men out from each direction. It was of the toughest jobs in my thirty-two years as a fireman. The work was so exhausting and the heat so intense during the search that the men had to be continually relieved by their colleagues.'

He described the assistance given by the shipyard's own safety team as 'magnificent.'

The story named the ship as the Toronto Star instead of the Toronto City. Perhaps in a rush to meet the newspaper's deadline, the reporter made a mistake in the ship's name.

Ships being fitted-out at Doxford's.

Strength In Numbers

For many years everyone in the steel trades were on piece work – you were paid by how much you did. People seemed to be more concerned about earning their wages than the conditions they worked in.

You used to have all the individual trades looking after their own interests and being very parochial. As years went by people started to realise that if they all stood together everyone was better off and everyone gained. So when the company had to talk about pay rises they didn't have to go around ten different groups. Austin & Pickersgill's had a strong shop stewards' committee and we represented everyone in the yard and so you had a stronger base to argue from. When you spoke to management they knew you were representing every worker in the yard. You had the strength and backing of the whole yard. That was especially true when arguing for better conditions and they improved in the 1970s and '80s beyond recognition. I think companies did start to realise that it was in their own interests to keep the level of accidents down. Improved conditions brought improved production.

Kenny Downes

How We Did It

It was hard work in the shipyards when I started in the 1930s. Conditions were bad and safety wasn't considered. Pickersgill's were one of the first yards to introduce a lot of new safer conditions. People from other yards would come to see how we did it.

Tommy Bell

Shipbuilding under floodlights at Austin & Pickersgill's, *circa* 1980. A SD14 is under construction on the berth.

Little Billy

The Quiet Lad

By the early 1970s Thompson's was building the big 'uns – 150,000 ton bulk carriers and we were working from staging at tremendous heights. I had an awareness for taking extra care. Falling from the deckhead staging to the tank top below left no chance of survival. Thompson's did not have safety nets across the holds like Swan Hunter's where I later worked. I'm not ashamed to say that as a 21-year-old at Thompson's I developed a fear of losing my life by falling or having something fall on my head from a great height. Hard hats weren't commonly worn in those days. Perhaps it is a paradox that I don't consider myself afraid of heights. I didn't have that fear in other yards after I left Thompson's.

An accident occurred early in 1973 which hit home hard the stark reality of the dangers to which we were being exposed. Small cabins had recently been provided for us to have our bait. Before this we would find a burner and his machine to keep us warm while we ate our bait on the staging under the deck. Billy Burlinson, better known as 'Little Billy', was a burner who had his bait in our cabin on the deck. He was a quiet lad who didn't get involved in the petty arguments, irritations and politics of an industrial bait cabin where men are crowded together. One cold morning in February 1973, Billy was given a job in a top saddle tank shortly before the dinner hour. The wooden manhole cover on which he was standing cracked and broke and Billy fell through the manhole down between the double skin bulkhead and on to the tank top 70 feet below. We heard the following day that he had died in hospital. Billy was twenty-six and married with a young daughter. Billy's death was shocking. He was such a nice lad.

Peter Gibson

A Terrible Shock

I would like to say that the shipyards and also the pits are not missed by families who have lost their loved ones in these dangerous industries. It is a terrible shock to hear that your husband has had an accident at work and later to be told that he has died.

On the day of Billy's funeral a mass of workmen surrounded St Peter's Church; Bob Maw, Bobby Reah, Alan Brown and Billy Carney, who were his friends, carried the coffin into the church. After the service the burial took place at Mere Knolls Cemetery.

The workmen of JL Thompson's had been shocked by the death and gathered a considerable amount of money which was presented to me by the men of the union. There was also money raised by a charity concert given by Bobby Knoxall – a first rate Sunderland comedian.

Today the River Wear lies idle and in the place of JL Thompson's is the University of Sunderland's St Peter's Campus which teaches the new ways of knowledge in computers which I think is a better start to life for the young workers of today.

Margaret Thynne (formerly Burlinson)

WARTIME

Record Output … Bomb Damage … Mrs Churchill … The King And Queen … Wartime Apprentices … Women Workers …

Two wartime apprentices at Pickersgill's –
Alan Whalam (left) and Norman Young.

In March 1945 the *Sunderland Echo* published the figures for the wartime output of the Wear yards. Between September 1939 and September 1944, 245$^{1}/_{2}$ ships were built in Sunderland. The half a ship was a new fore end for an oil tanker which had been damaged. The figures for the nine yards on the Wear were:

	Vessels	Gross Tonnage
W. Doxford & Sons	71	481,601
Jos. L. Thompson & Sons	40	277,697
Sir James Laing & Sons	30 $^{1}/_{2}$	230,523
Short Bros.	27	179,002
Bartram & Sons	19	127,756
W. Pickersgill & Sons	20	116,814
S.P. Austin & Son	26	56,916
Shipbuilding Corporation	4	28,342
J. Crown & Sons	8	3,688
Total	245 $^{1}/_{2}$	1,502,339

Six At A Time

I was eighteen when I was put on hand-burning with oxy-acetylene at Doxford's during the war. I would be sent to the fitting-out quays and there would be four ships in the river at Pallion, one down Palmer's Hill and one up at the quay. Six at time were being fitted-out. At Doxford's there were six berths and so every two or three weeks you were on a different ship. It would take about six weeks from laying the keel to launch. Of course, they weren't completely finished, they would go off to the quay for fitting-out.

Harry Gibson

Boys at the Corporation Yard, *circa* 1946. Left to right: Eric Ridley, Jimmy Smith, Tucker Brown, - , - .

Ready For Anything

In some ways Messrs Pickersgill's contribution to the magnificent wartime effort of Wear shipbuilders is especially notable and interesting.

The firm has had the distinction of being selected to build special new types of vessel for the Royal Navy and they have set about the job boldly and successfully.

'My staff and workmen', said Mr Pickersgill, who represents the third generation of his family to conduct the business, 'have not been afraid to tackle any kind of job, even though they had no previous experience of much of the work they have been called upon to do. We have had real pride in turning our minds and hands to new tasks, and I think we can claim to have made a success of them.'

Sunderland Echo, 13th July 1945

The War Effort

In one year during the war I was at thirteen launches.

Tom Richardson

Extra Food

Working in the yards meant we got more rations. Every few months we would get extra tea and sugar ration.

Harry Gibson

Kept In Our Place

I served my apprenticeship during the Second World War at Pickersgill's. If you were capable of doing a job you just got on with it. Of course you never got men's wages. I worked right through the trade, from the construction side on the berth through to the outfitting side. One day I was working with another apprentice laying the deck. There was us two on one side and two men working the other side. We got our lugs clipped because we got ahead of them. It just wasn't on for boys to beat men at a job.

Tommy Bell

SHIPCONSTRUCTORS and SHIPWRIGHTS' ASSOCIATION

(No. /55) *Southwick* Branch.

APPRENTICE'S CARD (SHIPWRIGHT)

Name... *T. Bell*

Address....................................

....

Branch No. 17 .... Reg. No. NR. 27241

Date of Entrance.... 1-8-41

Rate of Contribution.... 3d Per Wk

J. B. Sanderson Chairman.

J. E. Johnson Secretary.

1941.

Tommy Bell's apprentice card from 1941. Tommy served most of his time during the Second World War when apprentices often did the work of the skilled men who had been called up.

Mrs Churchill visits JL Thompson's North Sands yard as part of her tour of Sunderland in April 1941.

The Sunderland Echo reported the visit of the wartime leader's wife:

Wearing a coat of grey Indian lamb, with a multi-coloured turban, Mrs Churchill was here, there, and everywhere, diving into frame-turning sheds, clambering through the yards, and peering through peep-holes in her eagerness to see all that was going on in the Wear's supreme effort to provide ships, ships, and more ships.

As she drove from yard to yard through riverside streets inhabited by the families of the shipyard workers, women and children stood at their doors, or clustered at street corners, waving and shouting words of cheer and encouragement. Cries of 'Good old Winston', and 'He's the man for 'em', were heard every few hundred yards.

Mrs Churchill first visited Short's yard at Pallion … The men raised their caps and cheered as she passed and got straight on with the job of building ships that are the first essential of victory in the great Atlantic battle …

Mrs Churchill's next call was at Doxford's where she saw big cargo ships in every stage of construction, from the keel-plate to the fitting-out quay. The roar and rattle of pneumatic riveters and the incessant clang of drilling machines and huge plates drowned the cheers which greeted her … Mrs Churchill had a special word for 14-year-old Lawrence Robinson, who had worked in the yard for three weeks as an apprentice driller. A tiny tot of a lad, with a shining ruddy face, the boy said to the Prime Minister's wife that he liked his job better than being at school …

At Joseph Thompson's yard the first vessel on the stocks that caught her attention was a large merchant ship which had been 'named' in white letters six feet deep, 'Winston'.

The aftermath of a bomb which landed on Laing's.

Bomb Damage

One day, when I was at Laing's, we heard a plane but we thought it was one of ours. Then I heard a crash and went through to have a look and there was a big steam wagon on its side. It crushed two men. Arthur Perry was one of the men killed. Two bombs had been dropped. The first one went straight through the roof and went off but the second didn't explode. Good job it didn't go off because it was a massive bomb. I'll never forget that day.

Bob Simpson

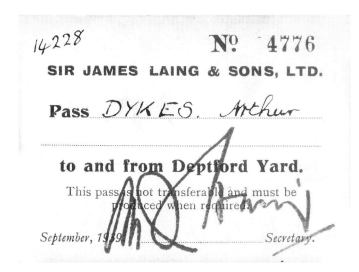

Left: Arthur Dykes' wartime pass to get him into Laing's. Shortly before Arthur started his apprenticeship in 1941 the yard was hit by a bomb. Arthur says it happened just before the men knocked off for their dinner. He knew Arthur Perry, one of those killed.

The King and Queen visit JL Thompson's, 8th April 1943.

The Sunderland Echo reported their visit to an 'unnamed shipyard':

Both their Majesties stopped to talk to a group of women workers. Mrs Page, aged 50, told them she was the oldest woman employed in the yard. 'The Queen asked me how I liked my work as a solderer', said Mrs Page, 'and I told her I liked it well. I said it was very healthy work, and the Queen said we all looked very healthy through working in the open air … Others to whom their Majesties talked in this group were Margaret Martin, Mary Davison and Martha Jenkins … The Queen had a word for one of the youngest girl workers, Irene Hodgson, asking how she liked her work in the general store … In the busy foundry the King and Queen saw as many women as men at work.

Bailing Out

At Pickersgill's during the war we built craft for the Royal Navy – corvettes, frigates, admiralty tugs. Admiralty tugs were the first prefabricated ships we built. You had a massive list of parts and every part was numbered. All the units were made in a factory and we just had to join them up and put the finishing touches to them. I went up the river in the first tug we built and it took in water so we had to bail it out. We later built minesweepers which had to be non-magnetic. They were constructed of aluminium with mahogany hulls. I sailed on one of the minesweepers up the river and that started leaking as well. We got as far as the South Dock and had to leave her there to be bailed out.

Tommy Bell

Many women worked in Sunderland shipyards during the Second World War and their efforts were vital in the fight against the enemy. The authors of the book Where Ships Are Born gave a very 1940s view of women in the workplace:

It is generally recognised that a shipyard, where much of the work is rugged and carried out under hard conditions requiring a good deal of toughness, is not a suitable place for women workers. There were no women working in the yards when war broke out in 1939, but about the beginning of 1942, when the supply of men was becoming very short, women started to invade even this sanctum of purely male labour. From then until the end of the war the women shipyard workers continued to give fine service.

At its peak the total number of women employed in the Wear yards rose to about 700. Whilst the majority were employed on various kinds of unskilled labouring jobs, sweeping up and generally making themselves useful, many did useful work as welders, burners, painters, red-leaders, crane-drivers, platers' helpers, and even as rivet heaters and rivet catchers. In the marine engine works on the river many women took up work on skilled jobs. Some of them excelled the men in tending machines.

Within twelve months of the ending of hostilities, very few of these women workers who had helped their menfolk of Wearside to build the ships to make certain of victory, remained in the yards. Most of the others had returned to their homes which they cheerfully left from 1942 onwards to do their bit for the country in rough and unfamiliar tasks.

Women workers chat to a nurse while eating their bait during the Second World War.

Noise, Wages & Bouchers

When I started at Laing's as an apprentice welder in 1941 the first thing that struck me was the noise. A lot of the racket was made by the riveters. When the first rivets of the day were put in flakes of rust fell down your neck. There were no ear muffs in those days. To communicate, everything had to be done in sign language.

I think my first wage was 13s 6d. There was a high rate and a low rate. You would take a piece of welding to the gaffer and if he thought you had improved he put you on the high rate. It was a good incentive to learn.

The second welders' gaffer at Laing's was called Chris Anderson and he used to send me out to try to get him 20 Cravens. Cigarettes were hard to come by during the war but what he didn't know was that I could get my hands on them straight

Pearce Gibson.

away. At the time I was living with my uncle who ran Bouchers (Oddfellows Arms, Trimdon Street) which was near Laing's. I would get the cigarettes from the pub but instead of going straight back to the yard, I would stay out for a couple of hours. When I got back to work I would say I had trouble finding somewhere that had the cigarettes.

Pearce Gibson

Arthur Dykes.

Hard Times At Laing's

During the war we worked in the double bottoms without electric lights. We crawled along the 4 ft x 3 ft opening on our hands and knees. When we reached the place we were working at we stuck a bit clay on the bulkhead and placed a candle in to work by. The conditions were terrible, with no extraction to take away the welding fumes, but we had to get on with the job.

We only had half an hour for our dinners during the war. I would run home to Ravensworth Street, eat my dinner and run all the way back.

I worked at Laing's from 1941 to 1984. Of the forty odd years, I spent twenty-six years on nightshift. Shiftwork suited me because I kept pigeons. I looked after them during the day and my brother took over when he finished work.

Arthur Dykes

ODD TALES

Sale Of The Century ... The Ludo School ... Sneaked Out ... Bait Time Surprise ... The Singing Caulker ... Paid From The Coal House ...

Men at Doxford's enjoy their 9 o'clock break. Left to right: Stan Peacock, George Elrick, Brian Donaldson, Ray Wilson.

Sale Of The Century

On 18th February 1931 a most unusual auction took place at Sir John Priestman's shipyard. It was of a cargo steamer which was ready for launching but had not been completed because the Norwegian company who had ordered the ship had cancelled the contract at a late stage. The auctioneer, Mr D.R. Pinkney said at the time, 'I have never auctioned a ship, in a shipyard before, but I think it is a very wise action on the part of the builders because it has provided buyers with a chance of seeing the ship for themselves. Sir John Priestman is what we on the North East coast dearly love – a practical shipbuilder – and has a very keen pride in the craftsmanship of his people. He has no apprehension as to the result of the most minute inspection of the ship.'

The bidding was started by Councillor J.G. Potts who offered £10,000. Mr Pinkney replied, 'It is very kind of you but which part of the ship do you want to buy?' This was greeted with laughter from the other bidders. The highest bid that day, £20,000, was below the reserve price so the ship was withdrawn. The vessel was eventually launched on 10th May 1933 despite still not finding a new owner. The builders felt she was so up to date that once fitted-out she would soon be bought.

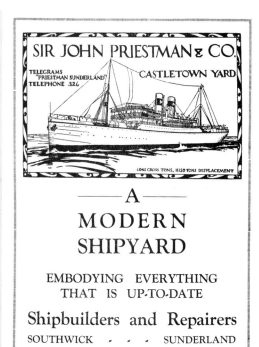

SIR JOHN PRIESTMAN & CO.

TELEGRAMS "PRIESTMAN SUNDERLAND" TELEPHONE 326

CASTLETOWN YARD

6045 GROSS TONS, 11150 TONS DISPLACEMENT

——— A ———

MODERN SHIPYARD

EMBODYING EVERYTHING THAT IS UP-TO-DATE

Shipbuilders and Repairers

SOUTHWICK · · · SUNDERLAND

An advert for Sir John Priestman & Co, shortly before the auction.

A Guy Named Joe

When Ken Douglas became Managing Director of Pickersgill's he made a lot of changes. He was a good man to work for and a bit of a character. He was once getting interviewed on television and he was asked, 'Do you know many men on the shop floor?'

He said, 'I know them all. I call them all Joe.'

Tommy Bell

Lying On The Beach

There were a few of us from Bartram's lying on the beach near to the yard and this bloke comes along and says, 'Do you know who I am?'

One of the lads says, 'He's a fella who doesn't know who he is.'

The bloke says, 'I'm Robert Bartram.'

So my mate says, 'Come and sit with us then.'

Ted Howell

A New Hat

A few years ago I was talking to a retired manager of a timber yard in Sunderland. He told me how in the old days of the shipyards even lower management ordered timber. One of the men used to say, 'I need a new hat.' To get the contract to supply the shipyard he had to pay up and buy him a new bowler.

Jackie Turnbull

TELEPHONE
5242-4

TELEGRAMS
THOMSONIAN, SUNDERLAND

ALL COMMUNICATIONS TO BE ADDRESSED TO THE COMPANY

JOSEPH L. THOMPSON & SONS LIMITED

SHIPBUILDERS
AND
REPAIRERS

ESTABLISHED 1846

YOUR REF.

OUR REF.

P.O. Box No.19.

North Sands Shipbuilding Yard,
Sunderland.

The letterhead of JL Thompson's, established in 1846.

Players Please

The store manager at JL Thompson's was a man called Bill Lowe who had recently came up from the south to work. Most of the men in the yard smoked Woodbines but he smoked Players Weights. One day he sent a young lad out for cigarettes. The lad asked him what he wanted if they had no Players Weights. He replied anything but Woodbines. The lad brought him back a bag of apples.

Billy Dent

Andy Pandy

When I was at Laing's in the 1980s the lads got up to all sorts of tricks. There was a blue hat (senior supervisor) who we called Andy Pandy. One day somebody made a dummy of him dressed in gaffer's overalls, blue hat and with a cigarette in a holder which was his trademark. A rope was put round its neck and it was swung over the side of the ship. He went mad when he saw the effigy of himself dangling about.

Keith Thomas

In The Picture

There was a gaffer at JL Thompson's who used to gather his men around him in the morning to tell them what work was on that day. He would say, 'Right lads, I'll put you in the picture.' So he ended up with the nickname – 'Rembrandt'.

Bob Palmer

Poor Managers

We had some poor senior managers at Pickersgill's. They were normally the people who had come into the yards from shoe factories or other businesses that had no connection with shipbuilding and they had no real experience of the industry. It was much easier to work with the local men who had worked their way up from the shop floor.

We were once talking to a personnel director who didn't have very much shipyard experience and we were telling him about the conditions we had to work under and trying to prove a particular point. Someone said to him, 'You don't know what it is like to work in double bottoms on a ship when you are crawling about in terrible conditions.'

He said, 'I don't have to know anything about ships to do my job.' That always stuck in mind and showed the type of people we had to deal with.

Kenny Downes

Caught Short

We launched the *Lord Glanely* from Pickersgill's during the winter of 1947. The frost had got to the launching shackles which gave way when they took the weight of the drag chains. First one shackle went then the others. Without the drag chains the ship ploughed into Short's Quay. In those days the shipwrights and apprentices would go out in cobles on to the river after the launch to collect wood that came down from the launchways. I was out in a coble waiting for the ship to come down – and it didn't half come down. The rudder ended up bedded into the quay. There was a toilet on the quay and the ship was heading towards it. As the ship got closer and closer there were shouts for the men to get out of the toilet. A few men came running out pulling up their trousers.

Tommy Bell

Slave Ship

Red-leaders in all the yards were characters. One day at Laing's, the men were coming off the ship at dinnertime. About seven or eight red-leaders came down the gangway roped together at the ankle by hemp rope. The gaffers were not too pleased with the appearance of this slave gang but the red-leaders weren't bothered. They were always a happy bunch.

Pearce Gibson

Painting The Town Red

There were always blokes in the yards doing a bit fiddle on the side to supplement their wages. There were a couple of brothers who worked as red-leaders at Laing's and the proprietor of a local shop or pub (I have forgotten which) hired them to paint his premises. The brothers used paint from the shipyard for the job. The boss thought the red lead was the undercoat and was shocked to learn this was the finished job.

Bob Palmer

Bairn Driver

My dad worked as a crane driver at Austin & Pickersgill's and during shipyard fortnight in the early 1980s, when I was six or seven years old, he took me into the yard. I still remember the ship they were working on at that time, it was the *Hunjiang*. He showed me around various cranes and let me work one that ran along rails up in the roof of the shed. Dad said, 'Not many bairns have had a go at driving a crane.'

Derek Laidler jnr

Left: Derek Laidler with his son, Derek jnr (right) and nephew Neil Marrin. Young Derek is sporting an A&P badge on his coat.

The Ludo School

Towards the end of 1973 I was employed for a short while at Greenwell's repair yard – the feast or famine yard. The conditions were filthy on those old ships and it was difficult to strike up an arc on account of the old paint and rust. On the lighter side there were the ludo games which took place in what appeared to be a boiler room on the quayside. I thought it was a wind-up when I first heard about it but there they were, grown men playing ludo for a dollar (25p) a corner. I eventually got a go but I didn't stand much chance against these 'professionals'. After throwing the dice I had to count out the spaces and heard the comment, 'Oh we've got an amateur here!' I observed the other three players knew the board so well that after their throw they knew where to place their counter without counting out the spacers. Amazing! The funniest part of the ludo school was that two of the regular players, who were well into their fifties, would take the board to the local pub and play ludo over a few pints during the Sunday dinner hour.

Peter Gibson

The entrance to Greenwell's repair yard, *circa* 1960. It was known as the 'feast or famine yard' and, for some workers, as a ludo school.

Black Outs

I worked at Pickie's when the power cuts were on in the 1970s. We just had to sit in the bait cabin until the electricity came back on. Someone said, 'I wonder if the power's on around the estates.' Another bloke said, 'It must be. I've just seen a bus with its lights on.'

Pearce Gibson

Wartime Shows

During the war I used to go to Doxford's canteen because they had shows on like *Workers' Playtime*. There would be comedians like Charlie Chester on. I was at school at the time so I had to sneak in. I would sit and watch the show while the men were having their dinners.

Jean Fowler

Horror Shocker

One day when I was serving my time at JL Thompson's in the late 1950s most of the apprentices decided to bunk off work. There was a good picture on the Royal Theatre in Bedford Street which we all wanted to see. As we were watching *Creature From The Black Lagoon* a message came up on screen, 'Will all JL Thompson apprentices report back to work.'

Billy Dent

Sneaked Out

I wasn't a shipyard worker but the firm I worked for sometimes did contract work in the yards. One day I was at Pickie's where my brother-in-law worked. It was about 11 o'clock and I had just finished my job and was packing up when he came up to me and said, 'Any chance of helping me get out?' So we sneaked him into the back of our van pretending he was one of our workers. I was never stopped at the gate so we got straight out. I dropped him off at Stoney Lane and he had the rest of the day off.

Billy Smith

A poster for *Creature From The Black Lagoon*. When apprentices from JL Thompson's watched the film at the Royal in Bedford Street they got a bigger shock than they were expecting.

Austin & Pickersgill's football team, 1972. Back row, left to right: Jimmy Thompson, Bryan Rackstraw, Kenny Downes, Frankie Russell, George Russell, Mickie MacKenzie, Joe Dow, George Foster, Tommy Walker, Denis Trout, Norman Atkinson. Front row: Bobby Taylor, Eric Downes, Alan Philliskirk, Alan Watson, Tommy Hume.

Singing Caulker

Joe Dow was known as the 'Singing Caulker'. As well as working at Austin & Pickersgill's he would sing around the clubs. He once appeared on an early Tyne Tees programme with Jimmy Saville.

Bryan Rackstraw

Lasting A Lifetime

At Pickie's in the late 1970s there was a chart on the wall showing different sorts of safety boots. I was thinking which ones to get when a welder called Peter Newton, pointing to a certain type, said, 'Get a pair of them son, they'll last you a lifetime. I've had three pairs.'

Stu McSween

Empire Entertainment

Big union meetings used to be held at the Empire Theatre. On stage one of the top union officials said there were allegations that he was a firm's man. He told the packed audience, 'If I find these alligators there'll be hell on.'

John Potts

From Russia For Cash

In the 1960s Russian sailors used to be regular visitors to Sunderland. They used to sell thick hard-wearing check shirts to the men in Bartram's. It was the only way they could get cash to spend in the pubs in the East End.

Peter Martin

Bait Time Surprise

When we were on nightshift at JL Thompson's we used to take cans of food in to heat up at bait time. One of the welders, Billy 'Mooney' Lawson, was a real character. He used to take all the labels off the tins so nobody knew whose was whose or what they were getting. Some used to take just tins of rice in and ended up with beans and hot dogs.

Billy Dent

Can I Have A Lift?

The shipyards were a real trading place – you could get anything. One of the lads once bought half a pig. He lived up at Doxford Park and so asked a lad who lived near him if he could have a lift home that night. They didn't get on very well and the other lad said, 'I'll give the pig a lift but not you.'

Kenny Downes

Afters

While at Laing's in the late 1970s the bait cabin provided a respite from work. One day a lad called Bobby Bisto opened his Tupperware sandwich box to find his wife had poured a tin of soup into it because they had been arguing the night before.

Mickey Stephenson

Workers at Laing's in the 1980s. Left to right: Mickey McDermott (welder), Lol Crosby (welder), Gordon 'Gunner' Wilkinson (welder), Mickey Stephenson (plater), Vick Brookes (shipwright). The photograph was taken outside the bait cabin by Derek Frost.

Picture This

I worked at Bartram's in the 1960s as a photographer. One of my jobs was to transfer drawings from plans on to the actual metal plates. This was done by taking a glass negative of the plan up a twenty foot high tower where a light was shone through it down to ground level. The image was projected down on to the steel plate which was then traced with chalk and the metal taken away to be shaped to this outline.

A plane used to take photographs during sea trials off the North East coast.

One of my more unusual assignments was to take aerial photographs of ships during their sea trials. I was taken up in a light aircraft and made several swoops to take snaps. I remember one pilot was an absolute madman. He dived at the ship on apparent collision course and then flew between the derricks on deck.

Peter Martin

Paid From The Coal House

The marker off would be in charge of a squad of platers and he would get the money and pay the rest of the squad. I heard one particular marker off would make the men go up to his house to get paid and he would pay them from the coal house hatch.

Tommy Bell

Keep the Change
Young 'Un

When he was an apprentice at JL Thompson's, Harry Smith used to be sent out for cigarettes for head foreman welder Sol French. The gaffer always used to say, 'Keep the 2d change.' The cigarettes went up 3d but for ages the young lad was scared to tell him and paid the extra penny out of his own pocket.

Billy Dent

Tripe

Sol French once sent out an apprentice with a £1 note for a pound of tripe. He came back with a massive parcel. He had bought a £1 worth of tripe. He was never sent again.

Pearce Gibson

The Bike Race

The apprentices and men used to challenge each other to cycle from Laing's up the gas works bank without getting off. It was a hell of a bank to ride up and this was at the time the road was cobblestoned. Sometimes we used to stand and clap and other times there was money put on the riders.

Ed MacKenzie

In And Out At Laing's

At Laing's the gate opened inwards so at the end of the day, when the buzzer went, it was difficult to open them because the men were standing so close. Later they had a white line about fifty yards off the gate and nobody was allowed past there before the buzzer went. When we were let out I would run up the bank so I could get straight on to the bus.

If you were late getting to work they would stamp a hole in your clocking in card. One hole meant you were ten minutes late, two holes was twenty minutes and three was for half-an-hour. If you were more than half-an-hour late you had to see your foreman and hope he was in a good mood. If the foreman didn't need you that day, you went home and you lost a day's pay.

Kenny Downes

Ed 'Mac' MacKenzie with his adze – a shipwright's tool.

Shooting Yourself In The Foot

In the plumbers' shop at Laing's in the 1950s men used to collect waste lead. This would be melted down into bars, smuggled out of the yard and sold in the rag and bone shops. At the end of one day, when the men were gathered in front of the gates a couple of minutes before the buzzer went, a fella in the middle of the crowd had two lead bars hidden in his raincoat. One of the bars tore through his pocket and broke his toe. He was in agony but couldn't shout out because he would be discovered. As the man rushed out, the gateman found the discarded bar of lead.

Bob Palmer

Chopper

I had a pair of spectacles which were the Glen Miller type. One day I walked into the joiners' shop at Laing's and one of the lads knocked them off with a bit of wood and they were smashed to smithereens. So I picked up a chopping axe and threw it at him. It flew past him and just missed some men building a wood coble. That's how I got the nickname 'Chopper'. Nearly all the lads had nicknames in the yards.

Ed MacKenzie

The Cowboy

There was a welder in the 1960s known as 'Cowboy'. He would come to work on a bike with reins on it and called his welding rods 'flaming arrows'.

Bryan Rackstraw

THE END

The Final Years ... Ferries In The River ... The Campaign To Save The Yards ... The Last Day ... Demolition ... Today ...

The shop stewards' committee of Austin & Pickersgill's with Sunderland North MP, Bob Clay, during the campaign to save the yards in the late 1980s. Left to right: Kenny Downes, Peter Callaghan, Jim Baldwin, Dougie Combe, Bob Clay, Tony Carty, Mickey Deary, Bob Woodhouse, Bobby Row, Brian Tate, Danny Morgan.

The view from a car ferry launched from Austin & Pickersgill's. The ship was one of the last built on the Wear.

The story of the closure of Sunderland's shipyards in 1988 can be told no better than by the men who were part of the Save Our Shipyard Campaign. Peter Callaghan, Jim Baldwin and Kenny Downes – on behalf of the Austin & Pickersgill's shop stewards' committee – take up the story.

The Final Years

There was an open book for redundancies at Austin & Pickersgill's in the later years and a lot of older men had taken advantage of this. So we had a much younger workforce with an average age in their mid thirties. These lads had families and didn't want redundancy – they wanted to work. They should have had a bright future but it wasn't to be. The last few years were absolutely terrible because of all the speculation over our future.

In 1988, when the yard was running down, Austin & Pickersgill's had a policy that nobody would be made redundant – they could volunteer if they wanted to – but we would try and find another job for everyone who wanted one and re-train them if they needed it. No-one would be forced out of the yard.

Kenny Downes

The Last Ships

The last ships built on the Wear were the ferries. We got an initial order for four ferries which later became an order for twenty-five. They proved to be good vessels – fifteen were built and sold and are still working. I think the owner had a good idea for these ferries but didn't have a lot of capital. He thought he would get them built and then sell them off the peg but he suffered from poor cash flow which had a knock-on effect to our yards.

There was a lot of uncertainty in the industry during 1988. In the April, the Govan yard on the Clyde was sold. Later, during a debate in Parliament, the then Minister for Trade and Industry Kenneth Clarke said that buyers were now welcome to come in for the other yards. With all this uncertainty the shops stewards' committee called mass meetings of the workforce at the Empire to talk about what we were going to do. The campaign to save the yards was now underway.

Peter Callaghan

The Campaign

We were clinging on to any hope we could. At one point we thought we were going to get an order from Cuba and that became our big hope to save the yards. But at the same time we thought the government was against us and even if we put the best bid in we wouldn't get it. It was always the intention of the government to close the shipyards. It was about dogma and not common sense. Near the end it was all about politics. There was wheeling and dealing in board rooms, cabinet offices and in Brussels. We were just pawns in a big game.

We went down to lobby Parliament on more than one occasion and we met a lot of Ministers. I was in the House of Commons once when Kenneth Clarke stood up and said, 'I don't see a future for shipbuilding in this country.'

I turned to one of my friends and said, 'Well, we couldn't get a clearer picture than that.'

It didn't matter how much you put your arguments across no-one was listening. But the deal was done and shipbuilding was finished.

Kenny Downes

The final ships built in Sunderland lie idle on the Wear in the late 1980s.

The Closing Date

The date the yards were going to close kept being put back. At one time, they were due to close in October 1988 but at that point Mrs Thatcher was in Poland talking to Lech Walesa. So the government put back the date because it would have been embarrassing for the Conservatives to close Sunderland's yards when Thatcher was saying to Walesa what a good job he was doing at his shipyard. The yards eventually closed on 7th December 1988

Jim Baldwin

The Last Day

On the day the yards closed Tony Newton, who was now the Minister for Trade and Industry, made the announcement at about 3.40 in the afternoon. An hour before that I got a phone call from Bob Clay saying it was going to happen. I phoned the personnel director and told him but he didn't believe me – he said they would have been informed by British Shipbuilders. So I knew the yards were going to close before the company's board of directors.

Peter Callaghan

Where Was Our Future?

The decision to close the yards seemed to fly in the face of predictions of experts all over the world. Everyone was saying that there would be an upturn in shipbuilding and if we could just get over this bad patch there would be a future for the yards. But the decision had been made. Austin & Pickersgill's was a magnificent complex and it was flattened. In one way, when we knew the yards were going to close, it was a relief that the uncertainty was gone.

Kenny Downes

The *Challenger* – the last ship launched from JL Thompson's.

The *Stenna Wellservicer* at the Manor Quay. The maintenance ship for the North Sea oil fields was one of two built at Doxford's in the mid 1980s.

The importance of shipbuilding to Sunderland is graphically illustrated in the book Where Ships Are Born. One section describes the grim times suffered on Wearside when the yards were closed during the 1930s Depression. It is as poignant today as it was when written fifty years ago.

Skilled craftsmen who took a justifiable pride in their work, and whose work was the pride of their employers and owners of the ships they built, had to remain idle. There was no possible chance of them finding other jobs. The dole took the edge off the poverty into which thousands of families were plunged, but it was accompanied by the means test, which was bitterly resented. It meant that hard working and respectable men, the best type of working men, had to use up their savings, and, if they owned their own cottage – as many of them did – mortgage their dwellings before they could claim the uncovenanted employment benefit or draw out-relief.

Families were broken up. The more enterprising and younger workmen sought jobs elsewhere, or changed into other and less precarious occupations. There was much migration to the prosperous Midlands and the South.

Sunderland lost – for good, in many cases – some of her most skilful sons. In the shipyards grass grew in the berths; machinery and plant stood idle. In the town the streets were full of men filling in their time – after 'signing the book' at the employment exchanges – by wandering up and down. Without the background of humming noise of hammering and pneumatic riveting which strikes the ear of a stranger to Sunderland, but which is taken for granted by the native Wearsider when times are normal, and the yards are busy, the town itself seemed strangely silent as the shipyards themselves.

Austin & Pickersgill's in the early 1980s. This state of the art shipbuilding complex was demolished in 1991 and now a business and retail park occupies the land. Only the fitting-out quay and the nearby sheds remain.

A £45 million pound package of government and European money was given to Sunderland to redevelop the former shipbuilding sites at Southwick and the North Sands. As part of that deal shipbuilding would have to cease in Sunderland and a five year moratorium – later increased to ten years – was imposed. That moratorium comes to an end in 1999.

The Workforce Is Still Here

Pallion Engineering Limited acquired ownership of the yard in July 1991. We got our first order in the December of that year which were ducts for a power station. Orders followed for off shore work making us reasonably successful and secured an order book until the third quarter of 1993. However, for a number of reasons we got ourselves into some trouble. In late 1992 we thought the best thing to do was to finish off what we were contractually employed to do, run the workforce down and then wait for January 1994 when the five year moratorium on shipbuilding on the Wear would come to an end.

At the beginning of 1994 we applied to the DTI to return to ship related work and were turned down. The reasons we were given were the 'Seventh Shipbuilding Directive' which made provisions for a moratorium of a second period of five years to be implemented – therefore ensuring Sunderland could not build ships until 1999.

After 1999, when the moratorium is lifted, we can do as we wish. We don't want to build up people's hopes that shipbuilding will ever return to the Wear but we have the facility here in Pallion to bring back shipbuilding if conditions are right.

The workforce is still here in Sunderland to build ships. I think there are lots of people out there who are in their mid fifties who have the skills and the talent but have probably lost their confidence. If they were given another chance to work in the yards – I think they would come back.

Peter Callaghan

The Pallion yard in April 1998.

The Biggest Shipbuilding Town in the World

The former shipyard of JL Thompson's with St Peter's Church in the background. The land around the old yard has now been redeveloped with the National Glass Museum and Sunderland University occupying the site. This continues a 1300 year tradition of glass-making and learning on the banks of the River Wear. Former shipyard worker Doreen Robson says the banks of the Wear are blooming, 'The Glass Centre, the university, the housing complexes, the yacht club, the marina – not forgetting the Stadium Of Light – are heart-warming experiences. The hard work, ideas and enthusiasm of so many people have made this possible and seeing the results is very cheering. I hope the youngsters of today and future generations get as much pleasure from all these new improvements to the banks of the River Wear – hopefully some more jobs too – as we did fifty years ago when starting work in a Sunderland shipyard.'

The People's History

To receive a catalogue of our latest titles send a large SAE to:

The People's History Ltd
Suite 1
Byron House
Seaham Grange Business Park
Seaham
County Durham
SR7 0PY

www.thepeopleshistory.co.uk